4TH BIBLE READING MARATHON

A 26-WEEK TOPICAL BIBLE READING SCHEDULE

Our God, ...An Awesome God!

How awesome is the Lord Most High
the great King over all the earth! (Psalm 47:2)

THE BIBLE READING MARATHON PLAN

The Bible Reading Marathon was designed to encourage regular reading of the Bible.

We believe the Bible is the inerrant, inspired Word of God.

We believe regular reading of the Bible builds faith in God.

We believe that the Christian's life is faith in action.

We believe regularly reading the Bible should be a habit for a faithful Christian.

ACKNOWLEDGEMENTS

Copy Reviewers: Debbie Paine
Marie Weeks
Kevin Boyd
Growing Panes, Articles: G. R. Holton
Cover Photo: John Klimko

ORDER OF CONTRIBUTORS

G. R. Holton
John Hunt
Byron Brown
Myra Anderson
Don Seat
Carrie Seat
Homer Anderson
Francine Coppage
Toni Webb
Kenny Holton
Bryan Jarvis
Albert Little
Marilyn & John King
Richard Hamlen
Jerry Deloach
Leon Weeks
Kevin Boyd
John Klimko
Debbie Paine
Mike Paine
Bill Malone
Cheryl & Donny Bryan
Ruth Harrison
Larry Jonas
Janet Brown
Marie Weeks

SPONSORED AND DEVELOPED BY THE CENTRAL AVENUE CHURCH OF CHRIST

304 EAST CENTRAL AVENUE - VALDOSTA, GEORGIA

PHONE: (229) 242-6115

4th BIBLE READING MARATHON

OUR GOD, ...*An Awesome God!"*

A 26-WEEK TOPICAL BIBLE READING SCHEDULE

Published by

GROWING PANES, INC.
3543 Raintree Drive
Valdosta, Georgia 31601

Contact: grholton@yahoo.com

ISBN: 978-0-9905499-3-2

ISBN-990549933

Printed by CreateSpace, An Amazon.com Company
Available from Amazon.com, CreateSpace.com, Growing Panes, Inc., and other retail outlets

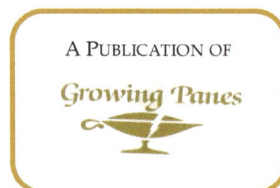

A PUBLICATION OF

Growing Panes

26-WEEK READING SCHEDULE

It's a Matter of Habit
"Our God...an Awesome God!"
Let the Race Begin!
10 Reasons to Read the Bible

A habit is defined by the dictionary as "an acquired behavior pattern regularly followed until it has become almost involuntary: the habit of looking both ways before crossing the street; or the habit of brushing your teeth every morning." Habit formation is the process by which a behavior, through regular repetition, becomes automatic or habitual. Strong habits become almost compulsory.

As the habit is forming, it can be analyzed in three parts: the __cue__, the __behavior__ and the __reward__. The cue is the thing that causes your habit to come about, the trigger to your habitual behavior. This could be anything that your mind associates with that habit, and you will automatically let a habit come to the surface. The behavior is the actual habit that you are exhibiting and the reward, a positive feeling, therefore continues the "habit loop." (from Charles Duhigg, *The Power of Habit).* A habit may initially be triggered by a goal, but over time that goal becomes less necessary and the habit becomes more automatic.

The ***Bible Reading Marathon*** is based on Duhigg's three-part "*habit formation"* formula:

A. *The Cue,* or trigger that begins the habit-forming cycle. The Marathon schedule includes posted scriptures, a time-table for reading, and beginning and end cues.

B. *The Routine,* or the behavior patterns that must become repetitive over time. On a regular (or daily) basis, you will repeat the same behavior, i. e., complete the Bible reading schedule.

C. *The Rewards,* or the positive, good feeling you experience for completing the behavior and completing the course. In addition, runners in the Bible Reading Marathon enjoy the knowledge of being blessed by pleasing God.

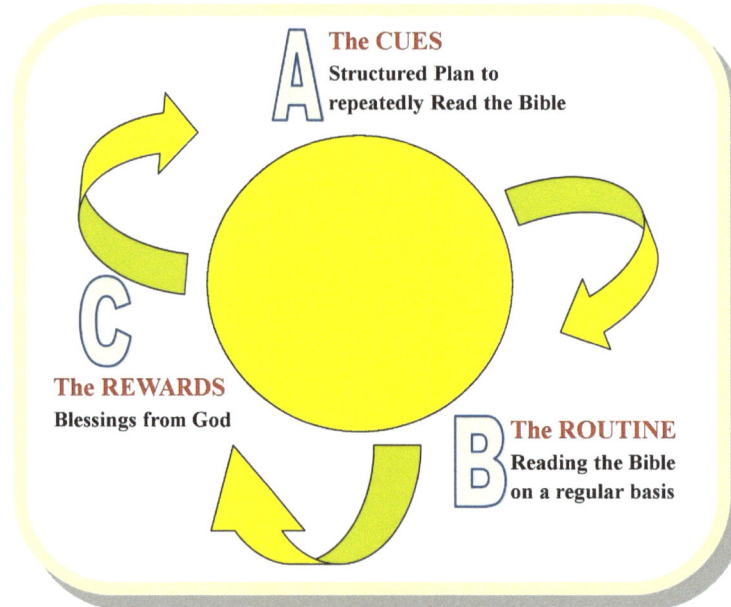

The Bible Reading Marathon is just *a tool* to help you develop the habit of regularly reading your Bible! Strong "good" habits are just as hard to break as bad habits. Regular Bible reading is a good habit. Use the next twenty-six weeks to form the habit of regular Bible reading!

4th Bible Reading Marathon: "Our God...an *Awesome God!*"

The modern ballad "Our God Is an Awesome God" by Rich Mullins captures the emotion of the vivid images of God revealed in the Bible with such expressions as:

> "There is thunder in His footsteps
> And lightning in His fists
> (our God is an awesome God)."

The Bible is the true story of our God. It reveals His character and divine virtues through the graphic encounters with the men and women of old. In the opening chapters of Genesis, God is revealed as a just God. One of His fallen angels is introduced as the perennial enemy of our God. The deadly nature of sin was painted in broad strokes in the experiences of Adam and Eve when they disobeyed our God.

But, the Bible also revealed the abiding hope of mercy by slowly uncovering God's divine plan of redemption. Introduced by the prophets of God, "a child was born" to bring that plan to the earth. Following the dark void between the testaments, "the light" began to shine. First, faintly as only an introduction by John the Baptizer, then as a clear vision from Pentecost (Acts 2) through the last letter of the New Testament. Finally, the majestic visions of Revelation reveal the full glory of our God. The lyrics of "An Awesome God" help bring that glory to our modern minds:

> When the sky was starless in the void of the night
> (our God is an awesome God)
> He spoke into the darkness and created the light
> (our God is an awesome God)
> Judgment and wrath He poured out at Sodom
> Mercy and grace He gave us at the cross
> I hope that we have not too quickly forgotten that
> Our God is an awesome God!

Any person can look into the starry sky, or gaze up at the giant redwoods and see the majesty of our God. His created world reflects His nature and speaks of His powers. But, only the regular readers of His Word can understand the mind behind the creation. The Bible says: "'For My thoughts are not your thoughts, nor are your ways My ways,' says the LORD. 'For as the heavens are higher than the earth, so are My ways higher than your ways, and My thoughts than your thoughts'" (Isaiah 55:8-9).

Without doubt, there is a huge gap between the thinking of God and our thoughts. God thinks on a level far beyond human comprehension. Yet He is willing to give us the tools to read His mind and begin to think like He thinks! God has not left humanity without a portal into His thinking. He inspired the books of the Bible to reveal His mind. Regular Bible reading is the process by which we mine those precious jewels from the very mind of God.

> "Our God is an awesome God
> He reigns from heaven above
> With wisdom, power, and love
> Our God is an awesome God"

That is the reason "Our God...*an Awesome God*!" has been selected as the theme for this year's Bible Reading Marathon. The Bible reveals his "wisdom, power, and love". More than that, he *currently* "reigns from heaven above"! God is alive! (grh)

> 12 ¹Therefore, since we are surrounded by such a great cloud of witnesses, let us throw off everything that hinders and the sin that so easily entangles. And let us run with perseverance the race marked out for us, 2 fixing our eyes on Jesus, the pioneer and perfecter of faith. For the joy set before him he endured the cross, scorning its shame, and sat down at the right hand of the throne of God. (Hebrews 12:1-2 NIV)

Let the Race Begin!

Make a Commitment!

I do hereby make the personal commitment to "run" in the Bible Reading Marathon.

(Signed): _____

Mark below which "Track" you will run!

☐ **INSIDE TRACK:** (Reading Time: 1-3 minutes each day)
- ♦ If you do not think you have the time or discipline to read more, start by regularly reading a few verses on the **Inside Track.**
- ♦ This track is also for the children who are just now entering "the Race."
- ♦ Read only the Scriptures in the first column of the schedule.

☐ **MIDDLE LANES:** (Reading Time: 3 -10 minutes each day)
- ♦ If you are a new Christian, or if you have not developed the habit of regular Bible reading, the **Middle Lanes** may be for you.
- ♦ The majority of "runners" will probably choose this track.
- ♦ Read *all the scriptures in both the Inside Track and the Middle Lanes.*

☐ **FAST TRACK:** (Reading Time: 20-30 minutes each day)
- ♦ The **Fast Track** is for the serious Reading Marathon runners who already have a strong habit of regular Bible reading.
- ♦ You are willing to dedicate the time and effort for 26 weeks!
- ♦ Read *all scriptures in all three lanes: Inside Track, Middle Lanes and Fast Track.*

Dedicate the Time...

Commitment to Run the Race: **Time and Track Choices**

10 Reasons To Read the Bible

I once read about a woman who willed her well-worn Bible to a nephew. Upon her death, he was so unimpressed with her gift that he tossed it in a box where it collected dust in the attic for decades. The story goes that after he died, his children were going through the boxes in the attic, found that Bible and discovered $50,000 in bank notes inside. Their father had a treasure in that book, and he didn't even know it.

Most of us won't discover money in a Bible. (Although, I still carry $2 in the front cover of mine that my daughter gave me in a Father's Day card fifteen years ago.) However, I suppose most of us likely have friends who would tell us that they have found a kind of treasure in the Bible that makes it well worth reading.

On that note, I've been thinking about reasons why reading the Bible is a worthwhile activity:

1) *It was written by and about people who had deep, spiritual insights.*

2) *It's a book of wisdom.*

3) *It's full of human interest stories.* For example, it includes tales about a person who tried to run away from God, a woman who rose from obscure beginnings to become a queen, a teenager who was sold into slavery by his brothers but who later became an Egyptian prime minister, etc.

4) *It's a "how-to" book, a human relations manual, on how to treat people and live a successful life.*

5) *It tells how ordinary people discover the courage and strength to cope with hardship and learn to live without fear.*

6) *It's a record of how others grappled with some of life's deeper questions, like,* Who am I? Why am I here? Why do good people suffer? and What has real value in the world?

7) *It explains how ancient women and men of faith began and deepened a relationship with God.*

8) *It purports to be a record of God's involvement in history and in the world.*

9) *It chronicles the beginning and growth of Christianity, one of the world's great faiths.*

10) *It connects readers with the life story of someone who is arguably the most influential person in history, Jesus.*

In his *Confessions*, Augustine of Hippo, a fifth century theologian and philosopher, tells of the time he once heard a voice that changed his life. The voice said: "Take up and read; take up and read." Thinking that the voice was referring to scripture, he picked up a Bible and began to read.

"Take up and read" sounds like good advice for us, too! One thing is for sure: we won't know what treasure awaits us inside that book until we pick it up and read it for ourselves. Happy reading!

-Taken from "Connect3Ministries" website and blog by Kerry Holton. "Like" Kerry on Facebook and receive his weekly encouragement blogs.

WEEK 1

This Week's Theme:

JEHOVAH: HOLY GOD

Dates: _____ - _____

INSIDE TRACK	MIDDLE LANES	FAST TRACK	
Monday:	**Monday:**	**Monday:**	Holy God
☐ Isaiah 5:16	☐ Exodus 31:12-32:14	☐ Psalm 47:1-9	
	☐ Leviticus 20:22-26	☐ 1 Samuel 2:1-10	
	☐ 1 Samuel 6:1-20	☐ Exodus 3:13-16	
		☐	
		☐	
Tuesday:	**Tuesday:**	**Tuesday:**	Idols and Our God
☐ Exodus 20:3	☐ 1 Chronicles 16:14-36	☐ Deuteronomy 32:15-21	
	☐ Ezekiel 14:1-11	☐ Jeremiah 16:17-21	
	☐ Acts 17:16-32	☐ Ezekiel 23:49	
		☐ Genesis 28:10-17	
		☐ 1 Corinthians 10:14-33	
Wednesday:	**Wednesday:**	**Wednesday:**	His Holiness Illustrated
☐ Exodus 3:5	☐ Isaiah 6:1-13	☐ 2 Samuel 6:1-9	
	☐ Revelation 4:1-11	☐ Acts 3:1-16	
	☐ Leviticus 10:1-3	☐ Romans 6:17-23	
		☐ 2 Corinthians 7:1	
		☐ Ephesians 4:22-32	
Thursday:	**Thursday:**	**Thursday:**	The Beauty of Holiness
☐ Psalm 29:2	☐ 2 Chronicles 20:13-22	☐ John 4:20-24	
	☐ Psalm 96:1-13	☐ 1 Corinthians 14:1-40	
	☐	☐ Deuteronomy 10:17	
		☐	
		☐	
Friday:	**Friday:**	**Friday:**	What this Means to us Today
☐ 1 Peter 1:16	☐ Matthew 6:24-34	☐ John 14:8-14	
	☐ Nehemiah 1:5-6	☐ 1 Peter 1:15-23	
	☐	☐ Hebrews 12:28-29	
		☐ Joshua 24:14-15	
		☐	

Growing Panes No. 401

The Word Brings Purpose to Life

I had just come back home for a visit during my first year of college. To my surprise, Daddy told me to get in the car because, "We are going shopping." Now Daddy was a hard-working welder. His hands reflected the dirty, greasy life he had chosen. But his *real life* started just a few years earlier when he followed mother's example and became a Christian. This contributed to the pride he felt that his son was planning to be a minister of the Gospel.

"If a man is going to preach the Word of God, he's gotta' look good" he told me as we entered the front door of Silverman's Dry-goods Store in Antlers, Oklahoma.

Inside Mr. Silverman reached into a glass case and brought out an entire box of Arrow white shirts! My purpose in life was christened when Daddy bought me that box of white shirts.

Jesus said, "Sanctify them by your truth. Your word is truth" (John 17:17-18). When we get into His Word, we will begin to find purpose and meaning for life. Sanctification not only sets us apart from sin, but it also sets us apart unto the divine purposes of God for us.

Dates: _____-_____	This Week's Theme:	WEEK 2

ELOHIM: GOD OF HEAVEN AND EARTH

INSIDE TRACK

Monday:
☐ Psalm 102:25-27

Tuesday:
☐ Psalm 24:1-2

Wednesday:
☐ Genesis 1:10

Thursday:
☐ Romans 6:23

Friday:
☐ John 17:3

MIDDLE LANES

Monday:
☐ Genesis 1:1-31
☐ Genesis 35:1-29
☐ Exodus 20:11

Tuesday:
☐ Psalm 50:9-12
☐ Psalm 95:4-5
☐ Haggai 2:8

Wednesday:
☐ Matthew 11:25
☐ Acts 4:24
☐ Acts 7:48-50

Thursday:
☐ Matthew 19:16-17
☐ John 3:15
☐ John 10:28

Friday:
☐ Matthew 6:10
☐ John 3:13
☐ 1 Thessalonians 4:16

FAST TRACK

Monday:
☐ Job 26:7
☐ Ecclesiastes 1:4
☐ Isaiah 40:22
☐ Isaiah 42:5-7
☐ Isaiah 45:18

Tuesday:
☐ Exodus 19:5
☐ 1 Samuel 2:8
☐ Psalm 148:1-6
☐ Isaiah 66:1
☐ 1 Corinthians 10:26

Wednesday:
☐ Exodus 9:13-16
☐ 2 Kings 19:15
☐ Psalm 33:6-9
☐ Psalm 66:4-5
☐ Psalm 90:1-2

Thursday:
☐ Luke 10:20
☐ Colossians 1:5
☐ 1 Timothy 6:12
☐ Titus 1:1-2
☐ 1 John 2:24-25

Friday:
☐ Matthew 6:20
☐ Matthew 24:35
☐ Luke 23:43
☐ Colossians 3:24-25
☐ Hebrews 5:9

God of Our World

Three in One

Dwells in Heaven

Ruler of the Universe

What this Means to us Today

Growing Panes
No. 402

Do Not Misuse the Scriptures

I had never been inside the famous Neiman Marcus Store in downtown Dallas, Texas. Parking was difficult to find. Tom drove up and parked his fancy white Cadillac on the side of a construction site just across the street. Nervously, I told him that we were going to get into trouble.

The site was One Main Place, a future 38 story building with 1.1 million square feet of space! Five levels were below ground!

"Just follow me," he said as he walked up to the edge of the deep hole and pretended to write on a clipboard. "Now, they have seen me, let's go to Neiman Marcus! They just think I am some important person with the city or the company and will not bother my car."

Scriptures can be misused. Some would use it as nothing more than a club to bludgeon others. Others would misuse it by saying, "You can make the Bible say anything you like" to undermine its authority.

The Bible is not just "some genie in a bottle" for our own selfish purposes. It is the Word of God which bears the image of God's name. "You shall not misuse the name of the LORD your God, for the LORD will not hold anyone guiltless who misuses his name." (Exodus 20:7).

WEEK 3

This Week's Theme:

EL OLAM: EVERLASTING GOD

Dates:
_____ - _____

INSIDE TRACK

Monday:
- [ ] Isaiah 40:28

Tuesday:
- [ ] Matthew 24:35

Wednesday:
- [ ] Hebrews 9:27

Thursday:
- [ ] 2 Peter 3:8

Friday:
- [ ] 2 Corinthians 6:2

MIDDLE LANES

Monday:
- [ ] Romans 1:18-25
- [ ] Psalm 90:1-10
- [ ] Isaiah 9: 6-7

Tuesday:
- [ ] Job 7:1-10
- [ ] Zephaniah 1:14-18
- [ ] 2 Peter 3:3-13

Wednesday:
- [ ] Job 14:1-12
- [ ] Job 14:13-17
- [ ]

Thursday:
- [ ] Psalm 93:1-5
- [ ] Psalm 102:11-28
- [ ]

Friday:
- [ ] Ecclesiastes 12:1-7
- [ ] Psalm 145:13-21
- [ ] 1 Timothy 6:11-16

FAST TRACK

Monday:
- [ ] Isaiah 55:1-9
- [ ] Daniel 7:1-14
- [ ] Revelation 1:7-18
- [ ]
- [ ]

Tuesday:
- [ ] Psalm 103:13-20
- [ ] Isaiah 40:6-8
- [ ] Mark 13:1-27
- [ ]
- [ ]

Wednesday:
- [ ] John 5:21-29
- [ ] John 11:17-26
- [ ] 1 Corinthians 15:35-45
- [ ] 1 Corinthians 15:46-57
- [ ] 1 Thessalonians 4:13-18

Thursday:
- [ ] Ecclesiastes 3:1-17
- [ ] Romans 14:11-14
- [ ] 1 Corinthians 7:29-31
- [ ] 2 Corinthians 4:16-18
- [ ] 1 Peter 4:7-17

Friday:
- [ ] Psalm 39:1-7
- [ ] Isaiah 40:21-31
- [ ] Isaiah 46:3-11
- [ ] 2 Timothy 1:3-10
- [ ]

The Eternal God

This World is Passing

Soul of Man never Dies

Time and Eternity

What this Means to us Today

Growing Panes
No. 403

The Bible is the "Living Word" of God

For over a century, the Brown Palace Hotel has been setting the standard for luxurious accommodations in Denver. At a cost of an unprecedented $1.6 million, the luxury hotel was built in the Italian Renaissance style on a triangular lot at the intersection of 17th and Broadway.

Henry Cordes Brown, who built the hotel, left his Ohio home in 1860, planning on striking it rich in California. However, as his family passed through Denver, his wife liked it so much, she reportedly said to him, "Mr. Brown, thou may press on to California if such be thy wish. I shall remain here."

The hotel *has never closed*, not even for a day, since it opened in 1892. Imagine that!

The Word of God is "living and active" (Hebrews 4:12). It will stand forever (Isaiah 40:8). Jesus nailed it: "Heaven and earth may pass away, but My Words will never pass away." (Luke 21:33). Eugene Peterson author of *The* Message translation, says, "Christians should not treat Scripture as a reference book to be dissected, but as the "living word of God" that bears relevance to the world today." The Bible *is* a "living word."

That Word is timeless. Imagine *that*!

Dates:	This Week's Theme:	WEEK 4
_____-_____	*EL SHADDAI:* LORD GOD ALMIGHTY	

EL SHADDAI: LORD GOD ALMIGHTY

INSIDE TRACK	MIDDLE LANES	FAST TRACK	
Monday:	**Monday:**	**Monday:**	God Almighty Makes a Covenant with His people
☐ Genesis 17:1-2	☐ Genesis 17:1-26	☐ Genesis 15:1-21	
	☐ Genesis 28:1-22	☐ Genesis 18:1-16	
	☐	☐ Genesis 35:9-15	
		☐ Genesis 48:2-16	
		☐ Exodus 19:1-8	
Tuesday:	**Tuesday:**	**Tuesday:**	God Almighty Supplies the Needs of His people
☐ Job 33:4	☐ Exodus 16:9-16	☐ Exodus 16:17-36	
	☐ Exodus 17:1-7	☐ Psalm 78:17-29	
	☐	☐ Hosea 11:1-4	
		☐	
		☐	
Wednesday:	**Wednesday:**	**Wednesday:**	God Almighty Defends His People
☐ Exodus 14:14	☐ Exodus 14:5-14	☐ Exodus 14:15-31	
	☐ 2 Chronicles 14:2, 8-15	☐ 2 Chronicles 16:1-10	
	☐	☐ 2 Chronicles 20:1-30	
		☐	
		☐	
Thursday:	**Thursday:**	**Thursday:**	God Almighty Guides His people
☐ Exodus 13:21-22	☐ Exodus 40:34-38	☐ Numbers 9:15-23	
	☐ Psalm 78:4-8	☐ Psalm 119:33-48	
	☐ Psalm 119:9-16	☐ Proverbs 4:1-13	
		☐ Isaiah 11:1-5	
		☐ Isaiah 48:17-19	
Friday:	**Friday:**	**Friday:**	What this Means to us Today
☐ Revelation 1:8	☐ Hebrews 8:8-12	☐ Hebrews 10:15-31	
	☐ John 6:29-40	☐ Hebrews 12:18-29	
	☐ 1 Corinthians 10:1-13	☐ John 6:41-58	
		☐ 1 Timothy 4:13-16	
		☐	

Growing Panes No. 404

The Word is the Power of God for Salvation

He did not become a Christian until he was in his late 80's, but he had attended services at the Westside church of Christ with his faithful wife for years. Many ministers held long Bible studies with him. Then, Willard Collins came to Muskogee, Oklahoma, for a Gospel meeting.

A courtesy visit was scheduled at the Smith's home. In the conversations, Collins asked him if he ever thought about becoming a Christian. "Yes" was his reply, but "I never really found the right time."

"How about tomorrow morning at 9:00 o'clock?" Collins asked. "I guess that would be a good time," was his reply.

The next morning all of Oklahoma was gripped in a terrible late winter storm. The roads were iced over. It was a *bad* day. But Mr. Smith kept his nine o'clock appointment. He finally obeyed the Gospel and became a Christian!

God's word will not return without results. For some the power-effect is immediate, for others it takes a long time to work. The power is in the Word, but the options for delivering that power are human. Like electrical transmission lines, weak human beings convey the soul-saving power of God! J.B. Phillips paraphrases Ephesians 1:19-20, "How tremendous is the power available to us who believe in God."

WEEK 5	This Week's Theme: *EL ELYON:* MOST HIGH GOD	Dates: _____ - _____

INSIDE TRACK

Monday:
- [ ] Psalm 68:34

Tuesday:
- [ ] Psalm 96:4

Wednesday:
- [ ] Genesis 2:7

Thursday:
- [ ] Joshua 23:16

Friday:
- [ ] Romans 5:17

MIDDLE LANES

Monday:
- [ ] Genesis 14:1-24
- [ ] Psalm 57:1-11
- [ ] Luke 9:38-43

Tuesday:
- [ ] Psalm 95:1-11
- [ ] Psalm 97:1-9
- [ ] John 1:1-5

Wednesday:
- [ ] Judges 16:1-31
- [ ] Ecclesiastes 7:28-29
- [ ] Amos 4:13

Thursday:
- [ ] Psalm 16:1-11
- [ ] Deuteronomy 7:3-5
- [ ] Deuteronomy 11:15-17

Friday:
- [ ] Acts 2:1-41
- [ ] Galatians 1:1-10
- [ ] Luke 10:25-37

FAST TRACK

Monday:
- [ ] Micah 5:3-5
- [ ] Psalm 68:33-35
- [ ] Deuteronomy 11:1-7
- [ ] Job 37:21-23
- [ ] Daniel 2:36-38

Tuesday:
- [ ] Genesis 1:1-31
- [ ] Exodus 18:10-12
- [ ] 1 Chronicles 16:8-36
- [ ] Philippians 2:6-11
- [ ] Psalm 135:5-7

Wednesday:
- [ ] Deuteronomy 4:27-29
- [ ] Job 4:1-12
- [ ] Jeremiah 32:26-29
- [ ] Ezekiel 28:1-10
- [ ] Hosea 11:1-11

Thursday:
- [ ] Jeremiah 1:15-17
- [ ] Isaiah 43:1-13
- [ ] Deuteronomy 13:1-18
- [ ] Joshua 23:14-15
- [ ] 2 Chronicles 7:11-22

Friday:
- [ ] 1 Corinthians 8:4-6
- [ ] Hebrews 1:1-4
- [ ] Acts 17:16-34
- [ ] 1 Corinthians 12:1-3
- [ ] 2 Corinthians 6:14-18

The Majesty of God

The Highest Preeminence

Man Compared to God

God and "Other Gods"

What this Means to us Today

The Bible Reveals the Majesty of God

Growing Panes No. 405

Some would say it was his medications or the effects of his ninety-plus years. Daddy's physical health had been going down for years. He had reached the point that one of us had to stay with him all the time, but his mind had remained active.

"There are millions of them...millions!" he blurted out as he raised himself up in bed and looked over at me.

"What are you talking about Daddy?" I asked with a degree of amusement, but also interested in what he was talking about.

"Angels...there are millions of them around the throne!" he said looking me square in the eye.

Perhaps a person whose life centered around the Bible just naturally focused on such Bible things at such times. True, it may have been just his subconscious surfacing. Just a daytime dream.

Or, maybe, *just maybe,* old Christians who are dying (and, possibly children!) are allowed to see the majesty of God. After all, the Bible does give two such detailed accounts of the prophet Isaiah (Isaiah 2) and John the Apostle (Revelation 4). Bible study *does* mold how we think about God. *Anyone* can "see" Him in the pages of the Book.

Dates:	This Week's Theme:	
_____-_____	*ADONAI:* OUR LORD AND MASTER	WEEK 6

INSIDE TRACK

Monday:
- [ ] Galatians 2:8

Tuesday:
- [ ] Mark 1:1

Wednesday:
- [ ] Exodus 24:7

Thursday:
- [ ] 1 Kings 1:37

Friday:
- [ ] Acts 5:29

MIDDLE LANES

Monday:
- [ ] 1 Kings 22:1-40
- [ ] 2 Kings 19:1-20
- [ ] Joshua 1:1-9

Tuesday:
- [ ] Matthew 1:18-25
- [ ] Mark 8:27-30
- [ ] Luke 4:40-41

Wednesday:
- [ ] Genesis 26:1-5
- [ ] Exodus 19:1-6
- [ ] Joshua 24:19-28

Thursday:
- [ ] 1 Samuel 1:8-18
- [ ] 2 Samuel 4:1-12
- [ ] 1 Kings 2:28-38

Friday:
- [ ] John 8:48-59
- [ ] John 14:15-27
- [ ] Ephesians 6:1-9

FAST TRACK

Monday:
- [ ] Proverbs 3:19-20
- [ ] Ruth 1:6-17
- [ ] Daniel 2:36-49
- [ ] Psalm 31:3-5
- [ ] Psalm 5:1-12

Tuesday:
- [ ] Luke 2:1-14
- [ ] Luke 9:18-20
- [ ] John 1:1-18
- [ ] John 6:60-71
- [ ] John 17:1-5

Wednesday:
- [ ] Psalm 119:33-40
- [ ] Matthew 28:16-20
- [ ] Mark 1:21-27
- [ ] Luke 11:24-28
- [ ] Jonah 3:1-10

Thursday:
- [ ] 1 Kings 12:25-33
- [ ] Genesis 18:1-15
- [ ] Genesis 24:42-61
- [ ] 1 Samuel 25:14-35
- [ ] 1 Kings 18:7-15

Friday:
- [ ] Romans 6:15-18
- [ ] Galatians 5:1-8
- [ ] Philippians 2:1-13
- [ ] Hebrews 4:1-13
- [ ] 1 Peter 3:1-7

Lord and Master

Christ as Lord

Obeying our Lord

Our Lord and "Our Lords"

What this Means to us Today

Growing Panes
No. 406

Being Submissive to the Will of Our Father

An old preacher story tells of a father who left a Last Will and Testament instructing his sons how to dispose of his properties after his death. The father dictated the smallest of details. A family house was to be built on a beautiful hillside overlooking the valley. The sons stood on the spot, looked out and remarked how wise it was of the father to designate this spot. A well was to be dug in a hollow where the hills came together. Again, a perfect place for a well, they thought, "Our Father was so wise!" Third, on a fertile field down the road just south of the house an apple orchard was to be planted. The sons stood on the location and looked across to a small one-room school house.

"We can't plant this orchard here," they said, "Children will come out of school in the afternoon, walk directly across the road, and pick the apples! No, the orchard should be placed in a back field far from the school," they decided.

Question: To which of the three instructions were they obedient to the Will of the father? *NONE!*

Jesus asked the question, "Why call me Lord...and Master... and do not do what I say?" (Luke 6:46). If we only do what the Word of God says *because we happened to agree with it,* we are not truly submissive to the will of the Father.

WEEK 7

This Week's Theme:
JEHOVAH NISSI: THE LORD, MY BANNER

Dates:
_____ - _____

INSIDE TRACK	MIDDLE LANES	FAST TRACK	
Monday:	**Monday:**	**Monday:**	God gave His People Victory
☐ Exodus 17:15	☐ Exodus 17:1-17	☐ Deuteronomy 25:17-19	
	☐ Deuteronomy 20:1-4	☐ Psalm 36:1-12	
	☐ Numbers 24:17-20	☐ Isaiah 13:1-6	
		☐	
		☐	
Tuesday:	**Tuesday:**	**Tuesday:**	Amalekites as Enemies of God's People
☐ 1 Samuel 15:2	☐ 1 Samuel 15:1-9	☐ 1 Samuel 15:10-33	
	☐ 1 Samuel 30:1-6	☐ 1 Samuel 28:15-20	
	☐	☐ 1 Samuel 30:7-20	
		☐ Esther 3:1-15	
		☐ Esther 7:3-10	
Wednesday:	**Wednesday:**	**Wednesday:**	Amalekites Symbolize the Sins of the Flesh
☐ Ephesians 5:3	☐ Genesis 25:27-34	☐ 1 Corinthians 6:9-20	
	☐ Genesis 36:10-12	☐ 1 Corinthians 5:9-13	
	☐ Hebrews 12:12-17	☐ Ephesians 5:1-17	
		☐ Ephesians 6:10-18	
		☐	
Thursday:	**Thursday:**	**Thursday:**	Banners Show Where God's People Belong
☐ Numbers 1:52	☐ Numbers 2:3, 10, 18, 25	☐ Psalm 20:1-9	
	☐ Numbers 10:11-25	☐ Psalm 60:1-12	
	☐ Isaiah 49:22-26	☐ Isaiah 62:1-12	
		☐ Isaiah 11:10 – 12:2	
		☐	What this Means to us Today
Friday:	**Friday:**	**Friday:**	
☐ Galatians 5:16	☐ Galatians 5:13-25	☐ Romans 7:18-25	
	☐ John 8:31-36	☐ Romans 8:4-17	
	☐ Romans 8:1-3	☐ James 3:13-18	
		☐ Revelation 19:11-21	
		☐	

Growing Panes No. 407

Faith to Stand Comes by the Word of God

In 1983, the Florida Gators were nationally ranked 5th and the Auburn Tigers were ranked 4th. The game pivoted around one play in the third quarter into a 28-21 win for Auburn. The Gators appeared to score when Neal Anderson carried in from 8 yards, but the ball was knocked loose and rolled out of the end zone. Official Billy Schroer called the fumble prior to crossing the goal line and awarded the ball to Auburn. Loud protests came from the Florida coaches and fans.

Schroer stuck with his call. After some delay, Auburn took possession. On the very next snap, Bo Jackson ran 80 yards for a touchdown. Arguably, Florida's hopes for a national championship hung on that one call. They finished the season as No. 3 with only one loss...to Auburn!

Reading the Bible builds faith in God (Romans 10:17). That inner core of self-confidence that supports us when everyone else seems to be against us! It is genuine integrity...character!

The call was right even though the official who made the call seemed to be the only one who believed it! Later, Billy got a call from someone who had a video of the play. Anderson *did fumble* the ball before crossing the goal line.

The Dwight D. Eisenhower National System of Interstate and Defense Highways (commonly known as the Interstate Highway System, Interstate Freeway System, Interstate System, or simply the Interstate) is a network of controlled-access highways that forms a part of the National Highway System of the United States. Its 47,856 miles make it the second longest highway in the world. The original system was to transport our fighting forces. Today, for many reasons, more people travel the interstate highways than all the others in America.

Have you ever considered how we rely on the mile markers and other numbered signs on the interstate highway? What child has not marked down the time to grandma's house by watching the markers on the side of the road! We have all been frustrated because we missed an exit number! The speed limits, distance-to-go, and even the direction we are going are monitored with numbers on the interstate.   These are meaningfully important numbers in our travels.

Reading the Bible is much like running by the numbers.   The Bible is filled with numbers. The most common are numbers like three, four, seven , fourteen and forty.   The number "7" is the most common besides the number "1."

Ed F. Vallowe (*Biblical Mathematics*, Olive Press, 1995) argues that "7" is a combination of the number "4" (a perfect world) and "3" (perfect divine number) meaning "earth crowned with heaven," the COMPLETENESS of God's universe. Consider that in Revelation where the word is found 54 times. There were SEVEN churches, SEVEN spirits, SEVEN stars, SEVEN trumpets, SEVEN vials, SEVEN dooms, and SEVEN new things. The number "7" is used over 700 times in the Bible.

In the Old Testament, we know the world was created in SEVEN days...and SEVEN feast days! The word "create" is used SEVEN times in the first chapter of Genesis. The author of Hebrews used SEVEN titles to refer to Christ: "Heir of all things," "Captain of our salvation," "Apostle," "Author of salvation," "Forerunner," "High Priest," and the "Author and finisher of our faith." Odd coincidence, the word SEVEN is used seven times in Genesis Chapter "7!" Jesus said we are to forgive SEVENTY TIMES SEVEN. He spoke SEVEN things from the cross.

SEVEN is a number that you will read over and over in God's Word. Tyndale's Bible Dictionary says it symbolizes completeness, perfection. It symbolized the completeness of creation in Genesis. The completeness of the sacrifice of Christ on the cross may be symbolized by His seven utterances, especially, "It is finished." In the Book of Revelation, the last book of the Bible, God's completed plan is symbolized with 54 SEVEN references.

The Bible is a completed message from our God. Written by forty men over 1600 years, this factual account of actual events, places and people shows us who God is and what it's like to know him. The golden thread woven throughout the Bible is a simple message: God loves you and wants you to have a trusting relationship with Him.

The Bible is God's Word. Reading the 39 books of the Old Testament and the 27 books of the New Testament, over time, will produce a belief in the God we serve. Faith comes by hearing the Word of God.

You have probably found your goal pace in running this race. You have selected a certain time during the day to read ... morning or night! You have started well; now you need to continue to the end. Use this mile marker to stimulate your anticipation of finishing the race.

WEEK 8

This Week's Theme:

JEHOVAH RAAH: THE LORD, MY SHEPHERD

Dates:
_____ - _____

INSIDE TRACK	MIDDLE LANES	FAST TRACK	
Monday:	**Monday:**	**Monday:**	God's Care of His People
☐ 1 Peter 5:6-7	☐ Psalm 23:1-6	☐ Isaiah 40:28-31	
	☐ Matthew 6:25-34	☐ Matthew 10:28-31	
	☐ Philippians 4:4-20	☐ John 3:16-21	
		☐ Romans 8:28-39	
		☐ Revelation 7:13-17	
Tuesday:	**Tuesday:**	**Tuesday:**	We are the Sheep of His Pasture
☐ Mark 6:32-34	☐ Ezekiel 34:11-15	☐ Psalm 100:1-5	
	☐ Matthew 2:1-12	☐ Matthew 26:17-31	
	☐ Mark 14:27-42	☐ Mark 6:32-44	
		☐ 1 Peter 2:13-25	
		☐	
Wednesday:	**Wednesday:**	**Wednesday:**	Under-shepherds, God's Shepherds
☐ 1 Thessalonians 5:12-13	☐ Ephesians 4:11-16	☐ Acts 14:19-23	
	☐ 1 Timothy 5:1-21	☐ Acts 15:1-35	
	☐ 1 Peter 5:1-11	☐ Acts 20:17-31	
		☐ 1 Timothy 3:1-7	
		☐ Titus 1:5-16	
Thursday:	**Thursday:**	**Thursday:**	Jesus, the Good Shepherd
☐ John 10:14-15	☐ Matthew 9:27-35	☐ Isaiah 40:10-11	
	☐ Luke 12:22-34	☐ John 10:1-30	
	☐ Hebrews 13:1-21	☐ John 17:1-26	
		☐ Colossians 3:12-17	
		☐	
Friday:	**Friday:**	**Friday:**	What this Means to us Today
☐ Matthew 9:36-38	☐ Matthew 28:9-20	☐ Matthew 25:31-46	
	☐ Mark 16:9-20	☐ Luke 10:1-17	
	☐ Ephesians 2:1-10	☐ John 21:15-19	
		☐ Romans 5:6-17	
		☐ Romans 10:14-15	

Growing Panes

No. 408

The Good Shepherd, Sheep and Wolves

Visitors to Ireland are impressed with the beautiful emerald meadows and the flocks of sheep with brightly painted spots on their hindquarters. Since wolves and other predators are not very prevalent in Ireland, sheep with different owners often graze together. In today's world, it is not unusual for them to use cans of spray paint to mark the sheep. Each owner has his own special "brand" and color. The sheep are then separated to their respective owners at shearing and breeding times.

The image of a "shepherd" and "his sheep" runs throughout the Bible (Psalms 23; John 10). Jesus is the chief shepherd. We are all sheep. Some go astray. Others are destroyed by predators.

One of the most dangerous images in the Bible is that of a "wolf" in "sheep's clothing" (Matthew 7:15). The idea is that of those who play a role contrary to their real character.

The Bible warns of such dangerous people pretending to be harmless. An enemy disguised as a friend! These are false guides. They lead many away to false teaching and immoral living.

Jesus knows his sheep by name. He leads them. They will not follow a stranger. He is their savior. Jesus is a good shepherd. He laid down his life for his sheep. (John 10). He will leave his entire flock, if necessary, for one sheep that is lost. (Luke 15).

Dates:	This Week's Theme:	WEEK 9
_____-_____	*JEHOVAH RAPHA*: THE LORD THAT HEALS	

JEHOVAH RAPHA: THE LORD THAT HEALS

INSIDE TRACK

Monday:
- [ ] Jeremiah 17:14

Tuesday:
- [ ] Proverbs 12:18

Wednesday:
- [ ] Psalm 147:3

Thursday:
- [ ] Psalm 30:1-2

Friday:
- [ ] James 5:16

MIDDLE LANES

Monday:
- [ ] Exodus 15:1-27
- [ ]
- [ ]

Tuesday:
- [ ] Exodus 16:1-36
- [ ]
- [ ]

Wednesday:
- [ ] Jeremiah 33:1-11
- [ ] 2 Corinthians 12:7-10
- [ ] Psalm 34:18

Thursday:
- [ ] Matthew 8:5-17
- [ ] Mark 9:14-29
- [ ]

Friday:
- [ ] Ephesians 6:1-20
- [ ] 1 Peter 2:21-25
- [ ]

FAST TRACK

Monday:
- [ ] 2 Kings 20:1-11
- [ ] Psalm 42:1-11
- [ ] Deuteronomy 7:11-16
- [ ] Jeremiah 31:12-17
- [ ] 1 Corinthians 15:50-55

Tuesday:
- [ ] Psalm 107:1-21
- [ ] Luke 6:20-22
- [ ] Matthew 14:13-21
- [ ]
- [ ]

Wednesday:
- [ ] Luke 6:12-19
- [ ] Psalm 103:1-5
- [ ] Isaiah 40:11
- [ ] Isaiah 40:28-31
- [ ]

Thursday:
- [ ] Mark 5:21-43
- [ ] Matthew 14:34-36
- [ ] Matthew 15:21-31
- [ ]
- [ ]

Friday:
- [ ] Isaiah 53:1-5
- [ ] Proverbs 4:20-22
- [ ] Revelation 21:1-4
- [ ] James 5:13-16
- [ ] 1 Corinthians 15:42-49

Bitter Waters Made Sweet

Bread from Heaven

There is a Balm in Gilead

Jesus, the Great Physician

What this Means to us Today

Growing Panes
No. 409

Bible Medicine Heals

Our 12-year old daughter had been in the Muskogee General Hospital for nearly two weeks running high temperatures with headaches. Our doctor came in and told us that she had a brain abscess and should be transported immediately to St. Francis in Tulsa. In the following days the diagnosis was confirmed, and unless a broad spectrum of antibiotic drugs worked, brain surgery was the only other option.

Wally Wilkerson, a fellow minister from another Muskogee church, came for a visit and heard the prognosis. "Let's go someplace and pray!" he asserted. Shortly thereafter our young daughter received the broad-spectrum drug cocktail ordered by the doctor, which was designed to fight the cause of the abscess.

Finally, after two weeks of the same regiment, poison-killing medicines and tons of prayers, our daughter began to recover. The fevers broke. Her healthy colors returned to her face. A smile came in the place of her tears. She was going to be all right!

The Bible says, *"Is anyone among you sick? Let them call the elders of the church to pray over them and anoint them with oil in the name of the Lord. And the prayer offered in faith will make the sick person well; the Lord will raise them up."*

Was it Wally's prayer or the doctor's drugs? A modern commentary on this passage may say "pray" and administer medicine, "oil." Regardless, the operative phrase in this text is *"the Lord will raise them up."*

WEEK 10

This Week's Theme:

JEHOVAH SHAMMAH: THE LORD IS THERE

Dates: _____ - _____

INSIDE TRACK	MIDDLE LANES	FAST TRACK	
Monday:	**Monday:**	**Monday:**	The Omnipresence of God
☐ Jeremiah 23:23-24	☐ Ezekiel 48:1-35	☐ Psalm 139:7-10	
	☐ Exodus 3:1-10	☐ Isaiah 57:15	
	☐ Exodus 33:1-23	☐ Isaiah 66:1-2	
		☐ 1 Kings 8:22-27	
		☐ Acts 17:22-25	
Tuesday:	**Tuesday:**	**Tuesday:**	God and our Future Planning
☐ Psalm 16:8	☐ Jeremiah 29:1-32	☐ Psalm 145:18	
	☐ Psalm 34:18	☐ Joshua 1:9	
	☐	☐ Deuteronomy 31:8	
		☐ Psalm 27:1-3	
		☐ Psalm 139:11-12; 23-24	
Wednesday:	**Wednesday:**	**Wednesday:**	Trying to Escape the Presence of God
☐ Genesis 3:8-10	☐ Jonah 1:1-17	☐ Amos 4:6-12	
	☐ Jonah 2:1-10	☐ Amos 5:16-19	
	☐	☐ Luke 15:11-32	
		☐ Psalm 11:4-5	
		☐	
Thursday:	**Thursday:**	**Thursday:**	Jesus is There
☐ Hebrews 13:5-6	☐ Acts 9:1-19	☐ Matthew 28:19-20	
	☐	☐ John 17:20-26	
	☐	☐ Acts 18:9-10	
		☐ Matthew 18:20	
		☐ Acts 7:54-60	
Friday:	**Friday:**	**Friday:**	What this Means to us Today
☐ Proverbs 15:3	☐ Psalm 139:1-6	☐ John 14:18-23	
	☐ Psalm 139:13-18	☐ Proverbs 3:5-6	
	☐	☐ Hebrews 4:13-16	
		☐ James 4:7-10	
		☐ 1 Peter 1:13-25	

Growing Panes

No. 410

Our Faith Defeats the Powers of Darkness

Virginia's cancer was in stage IV when she expressed to her husband an interest in "going to Florida and just sitting on the beach." Knowing that time was crucial for her, Bob loaded his loving wife into the family car, and they made the thousand mile trip from Oklahoma to the Gulf Coast of Florida.

We joined them on the beach. It was hot. The sand fleas were terrible. We were continually swatting the flies that buzzed our faces. This was *not* a pleasant experience for the rest of us!

But, Virginia just sat there in that recliner with *that smile* that never left her face with her clear eyes glued on every wave that came to shore. She *knew* the source of her faith, and nothing

would keep her from making this final contact with her God of creation...not even the dark battle she was fighting with the messenger of death!

The Word of God is the main offensive weapon we have to battle the forces of darkness (Ephesians 6:12). The trials in our lives will literally "sift us like wheat" (Luke 22:31). The Word equips us and makes us strong for any battle with the forces of evil, including death (1 John 2:14).

Virginia "left" (as Bob puts it) just a few days later, but the images of her strong faith and her vivid ability to "see" God will remain with all of us for a long time.

Dates:	This Week's Theme:	WEEK 11
_____ - _____	*JEHOVAH TSIDKENU:* THE LORD OUR RIGHTEOUS	

INSIDE TRACK	MIDDLE LANES	FAST TRACK	
Monday:	**Monday:**	**Monday:**	The Righteous One
☐ Psalm 129:4	☐ Jeremiah 33:1-26	☐ Jeremiah 23:1-40	
	☐ Psalm 4:4-5	☐ Psalm 17:15	
	☐ 2 Corinthians 5:20-21	☐ Psalm 5:8-12	
		☐ Hebrews 1:8-9	
		☐	
Tuesday:	**Tuesday:**	**Tuesday:**	Right and Wrong
☐ Proverbs 14:12	☐ Isaiah 5:20	☐ Exodus 20:1-17	
	☐ Galatians 5:1-26	☐ Matthew 26:41	
	☐ Ephesians 4:17-32	☐ John 3:19-21	
		☐ James 4:17	
		☐ 2 Corinthians 13:7	
Wednesday:	**Wednesday:**	**Wednesday:**	Justice
☐ Romans 12:19-21	☐ Deuteronomy 16:18-20	☐ Job 40, 41, 42:1-6	
	☐ Jeremiah 9:23-24	☐ Proverbs 21:15	
	☐ Romans 12:14-21	☐ Isaiah 61:8	
		☐ Micah 6:6-8	
		☐ Luke 18:1-8	
Thursday:	**Thursday:**	**Thursday:**	The Gospel and Righteousness
☐ Romans 1:16-17	☐ Matthew 26:1-13	☐ Mark 8:34-38	
	☐ Acts 20:17-24	☐ 1 Corinthians 15:1-8	
	☐ 1 Corinthians 1:10-17	☐ Galatians 3:1-29	
		☐ Philippians 1:27	
		☐ Colossians 1:3-7	
Friday:	**Friday:**	**Friday:**	What this Means to Us Today
☐ Romans 3:21-26	☐ John 10:25-30	☐ John 3:16	
	☐ Romans 8:37-39	☐ Romans 8:1-39	
	☐	☐ Hebrews 7:1-28	
		☐ 1 John 5:13	
		☐ Revelation 22:12-17	

Growing Panes
No. 411

I Want to be "Right"!

I had gone to Tulsa to hear the great Foy Wallace, Jr. As a young preacher, this man looked like *the very* prophet of God with his long white hair and stately *persona*. I did not want to miss a single word of his lesson, so I sat down on the front pew with my little tape-recorder and turned it on.

"Turn that thing off, young man," Wallace insisted, "I want you to hear the truth like it really is! People can make it sound different on one of those things!"

I turned my tape recorder off, and truthfully, I could not have recorded his entire sermon anyway. My recording tape was only for 45 minutes! He went for two hours... *without notes!*

We are impressed by people who seem to epitomize "the truth." In fact, one of the greatest challenges of the Bible is to understand some of the big words of truth. Words like "righteousness", which is used 228 times, mostly in Romans. The word literally means "to move in a straight line." It means to live or act in "the right way" for salvation.

But, what is the "right way?" The message of Romans (3:23; 5:18-21) is that *only* God Himself is "righteous." His character reveals what is absolutely right. He, *and He alone,* is the measure of moral right and wrong. That's the good news of the gospel of Christ (Romans 1:16).

WEEK 12

This Week's Theme:

JEHOVAH JIREH: THE LORD WILL PROVIDE

Dates:

_____-_____

INSIDE TRACK
Monday:
- ☐ Genesis 22:13-14

Tuesday:
- ☐ 2 Corinthians 12:9-10

Wednesday:
- ☐ 1 Samuel 17:37

Thursday:
- ☐ 2 Timothy 4:6-8

Friday:
- ☐ Matthew 6:25

MIDDLE LANES
Monday:
- ☐ Genesis 22:1-24
- ☐ Leviticus 25:2-4, 18-22
- ☐ Psalm 92:1-15

Tuesday:
- ☐ 2 Corinthians 12:7-10
- ☐ 2 Corinthians 13:3-10
- ☐ 2 Chronicles 20:10-15

Wednesday:
- ☐ 1 Samuel 17:31-50
- ☐ Genesis 19:1-26
- ☐ Matthew 14:13-21

Thursday:
- ☐ John 11:14-45
- ☐ John 20:1-18
- ☐ Acts 7:51-59

Friday:
- ☐ Matthew 6:25-34
- ☐ Matthew 7:7-12
- ☐ Matthew 7:21-27

FAST TRACK
Monday:
- ☐ Luke 18:1-8
- ☐ Genesis 45:3-15
- ☐ Exodus 30:1-20
- ☐ Joshua 1:1-9
- ☐ Hebrews 11:32-40

Tuesday:
- ☐ Job 4:3-4
- ☐ Isaiah 35:3-4
- ☐ Matthew 26:40-41
- ☐ Acts 20:34-36
- ☐ Romans 5:6-10

Wednesday:
- ☐ 1 Kings 19:1-18
- ☐ Judges 7:7-22
- ☐ Joshua 6:6-20
- ☐ Luke 18:2-8
- ☐

Thursday:
- ☐ Deuteronomy 34:1-12
- ☐ Judges 16:20-31
- ☐ Luke 16:19-31
- ☐
- ☐

Friday:
- ☐ Matthew 5:13-20
- ☐ Matthew 5:21-24
- ☐ Luke 12:22-31
- ☐ Luke 12:37-40
- ☐ Luke 12:43-48

God will Provide

Strength at Times of Weakness

Needs at Times of Want

Life in Times of Death

What this Means to us Today

Growing Panes No. 412

God *Will* Provide

Payday would not come from my grocery job until Friday. We had just enough money to make our rent payment early in the week and to give our usual weekly contribution at church. I was a second-year student at Oklahoma Christian College driving ninety miles to preach for the small church in Porter. All the way down, we talked about whether or not we should go ahead and give our meager contribution or not. We decided to go ahead and make our contribution and, if necessary, hold up the rent payment until payday.

We were surprised when we got to Porter to see my big sister, JoAnn and her husband Ed, who came over to hear her "baby brother preach." They took us out to lunch after church before saying their goodbyes and heading back home. As they got into

their car Ed handed me a $20 bill!

"We know you must be struggling going to school, and we just want to help," he insisted.

That twenty dollars was bigger on that day than they could have ever imagined! It was far more than we had contributed at church. It literally carried us through to payday...but, more than that, it taught us a lesson about *how* God *does* provide.

The Bible is full of inspiring assurances of how God will provide for his followers. (Matthew 6:31-32; Luke 12:24).

"And my **God shall supply all your needs according to His riches in glory by Christ Jesus.** Now to our God and Father be glory forever and ever." (Philippians 4:19-20).

Our God...*an Awesome God*   4th Bible Reading Marathon

Pacing with Patience...

Many marathon runners are familiar with the term "putting time in the bank," which is a simple way of describing a running strategy of running the first half of a race faster than the goal pace. The idea is to make up for the slower time during the second half of the race. However, a study reported in the *Journal of Strength and Conditioning* found that a *too fast* first half considerably reduced over-all performance, so much so that almost all the runners who started too fast failed to even finish the race.

You are now at the mid-way point in our Bible Reading Marathon. Several started out with a bang but have *bonked*! They just dropped out. Your dedication to the goal to develop a "Regular Bible Reading Habit" is being severely challenged. Your brain muscles are tired. Your mind keeps telling you to quit. Don't! Now is the time to face your resistance. Keep on reading!

In fact, Matt Fitzgerald, author of several books on training to run marathons, says, "Learning to properly pace yourself is the most critical skill a runner can develop." He notes that once you burn through the carbohydrates, the primary fuel for running, you will "bonk," or "hit the wall." The only thing that can prevent this, he says, is to pace yourself!

The Bible gives us some basic tips on how to pace ourselves:

> *Wherefore seeing we also are compassed about with so great a cloud of witnesses, let us lay aside every weight, and the sin which doth so easily beset us, and let us run with patience the race that is set before us, Looking unto Jesus the author and finisher of our faith; who for the joy that was set before him endured the cross, despising the shame, and is set down at the right hand of the throne of God.* (Hebrews 12:1-2).

Tip #1: *Get a running partner!*

There is a literal cloud of "witnesses" in this race. Pick out someone you know for support who is also running the BRM race. It likely may be an older Christian who is up-to-date in the readings. Ask him or her questions about some of the readings. Let your interactions build that supportive relationship you need.

Tip #2: *Remove any obstacles that keep you from being regular!*

You may need to change the time of day you would prefer reading. Just before bedtime may be a bad time. Like any good exercise program, you just have to dedicate a time to do it and then...DO IT!

Tip #3: *Keep your eyes on Jesus!*

Remember, this is not just reading a book, but reading THE BOOK! This is the story of the greatest story on earth. God became flesh and lived among us on earth. The Bible is a six-thousand-year history of how that happened. This is great reading!

Tip #4: *Keep the "finish line" in your mind's eye!*

Our journey with God may force us to climb the hills that seem insurmountable! We get tired. But the author of our race is also our finisher! He has promised that he will be with us all the way. Heaven is our goal.

Tip #5: *Keep following "Tip #1 #2, #3 and Tip #4"!*

Make it a *habit*! Repetition, repetition, repetition! In the lingo of marathon training, "Practice, practice, practice!" Keep on reading until it becomes so compulsive that you would not feel right if you had not read your passages for the day.

> *Take a few minutes to catch your breath, then get back in the race!*

MILE POST #13:   **SPIRITUAL REFRESH STATION**

WEEK 13

This Week's Theme:
JEHOVAH SHALOM: THE LORD IS PEACE

Dates:
_____-_____

INSIDE TRACK	MIDDLE LANES	FAST TRACK	
Monday:	**Monday:**	**Monday:**	A God of Peace
☐ Judges 6:23-24	☐ Judges 6:1-40	☐ Isaiah 48:1-22	
	☐	☐ 1 Corinthians 14: 26-33	
	☐	☐ 1 Thessalonians 5:12-28	
		☐ Romans 15:1-13	
		☐	
Tuesday:	**Tuesday:**	**Tuesday:**	Peace between God and Man
☐ Psalm 4:8	☐ Luke 1:67-80	☐ Psalm 29:1-11	
	☐ Romans 8:1-17	☐ 2 Peter 3:1-14	
	☐ Numbers 6:22-27	☐ 2 Corinthians 1:1-6	
		☐ Romans 5:1-11	
		☐	
Wednesday:	**Wednesday:**	**Wednesday:**	Peace between Man and his Fellow Man
☐ 1 Samuel 20:42	☐ Hebrews 12:1-17	☐ Romans 12:1-21	
	☐ 1 Peter 3:8-12	☐ Mark 9:38-50	
	☐ Romans 14:1-23	☐ Genesis 44:1-17	
		☐ Genesis 45:1-20	
		☐	
Thursday:	**Thursday:**	**Thursday:**	Jesus, the Prince of Peace
☐ John 14:27	☐ Ephesians 2:1-22	☐ John 14:1-17	
	☐ Colossians 1:9-20	☐ Isaiah 53:1-10	
	☐	☐ Acts 10:1-36	
		☐	
		☐	
Friday:	**Friday:**	**Friday:**	What this Means to us Today
☐ Psalm 120:7	☐ Isaiah 59:1-8	☐ John 16:1-33	
	☐ Psalm 85:1-13	☐ Romans 12:18	
	☐ Isaiah 57:1-21	☐ Romans 16:17-20	
		☐	
		☐	

Growing Panes
No. 413

The Bible says *"Pursue Peace"*!

The small country church had argued for years over personal opinions and other "doctrinal" differences. The disunity smoldered into anger, distrust and congregational division. Times were hard, so to maintain some degree of congregational civility they decided to divide, but to continue to use the same building. One faction would meet in the morning and the other in the afternoon.

This worked well for some time until someone opined that the "morning church" was using much more coal in the old pot-bellied stove than the "afternoon church". That was not fair. So, they solved the problem by instructing the coal-vendor to make two piles of coal. One for the "morning church" and the other for the "afternoon church."

The ridiculous nature of division was made clear in what one of the children was heard to say leaving Bible class: "One Lord, One Faith, One Baptism...and, two coal piles!"

Division is ugly. Churches ferment anger and hate when torn from the moorings of love established by Jesus. A lost world is at stake! Churches founded on this love must strive after peace.

Jesus prayed for the unity of His disciples (John 17). The Apostle Paul says we should "make every effort to keep the unity of the Spirit through the bond of peace." (Ephesians 4:3). The context of this passage shows that the character of the Christian to be humble, gentle, patient and tolerant can lead to peace.

Dates:	This Week's Theme:	WEEK 14
_____-_____	*JEHOVAH SABAOTH:* THE LORD OF HOSTS	

INSIDE TRACK	MIDDLE LANES	FAST TRACK	
Monday:	**Monday:**	**Monday:**	King of Heaven and Earth
☐ Amos 4:13	☐ 1 Samuel 1:1-11	☐ Zechariah 1:1-7	
	☐ Isaiah 6:1-13	☐ Malachi 1:1-14	
	☐ Psalm 24:1-10	☐ Jeremiah 20:11-13	
		☐ Jeremiah 27:3-22	
		☐	
Tuesday:	**Tuesday:**	**Tuesday:**	God and the Nations
☐ Isaiah 37:14-16	☐ 1 Kings 19:10-21	☐ 2 Samuel 7:22-29	
	☐ 1 Chronicles 11:1-9	☐ Haggai 2:1-7	
	☐ 2 Samuel 15:1-10	☐ Jeremiah 5:13-15	
		☐ Psalm 46:1-7	
		☐	
Wednesday:	**Wednesday:**	**Wednesday:**	The Soldiers in God's Army
☐ 1 Samuel 17:45	☐ Exodus 7:1-6	☐ Isaiah 24:1-23	
	☐ Joshua 5:13-15	☐ Zephaniah 2:1-11	
	☐ Luke 2:1-14	☐ Proverbs 18:1-10	
		☐ 1 Samuel 17:45-53	
		☐ Isaiah 19:1-25	
Thursday:	**Thursday:**	**Thursday:**	The Enemy
☐ Isaiah 5:15-16	☐ Isaiah 31:1-9	☐ Psalm 59:1-17	
	☐ Judges 4:1-24	☐ Amos 3:1-15	
	☐ Jeremiah 50:30-35	☐ 2 Kings 19:29-34	
		☐ Amos 5:14-17	
		☐ Psalm 84:1-12	
Friday:	**Friday:**	**Friday:**	What this Means to us Today
☐ Psalm 80:17-19	☐ James 5:1-20	☐ 1 Peter 1:10-25	
	☐ Isaiah 8:1-13	☐ Revelation 19:11-20	
	☐ Matthew 1:18-23	☐ Micah 4:1-7	
		☐ Luke 1:26-37	
		☐ Zechariah 8:1-8	

Growing Panes No. 414

"Think Past the Moment!"

Temptations are strong for viral young people. Some of the last words our children heard as they went out on a "date" were: "*Think past the moment!*" That admonition triggered in their minds the teachings they had learned at home and in Bible classes. In a sense, it was like telling them to "draw their swords" because they were going into battle with Satan.

The Bible is like a sword (Hebrews 4:12; Ephesians 6:17). The Word of God is a part of the armor of God to protect us as soldiers of Christ. We read it and study it to be safe from sin. Can you imagine a good soldier who had such an offensive weapon and failed to use it? Every time the Devil came at Jesus, He figuratively drew his sword with a "thus it is written" (Matthew 4:1-11). In the heat of battle, a good soldier wants a weapon that will be effective against the enemy. Good advice is to "Trust in the Lord with all your heart and lean not on your own understanding." (Proverbs 3:5).

"*Think past the moment*" when the battle is over and your faith has stood the test of temptation. Victory is sweet. Your peace is past understanding. Faith in God and the guidance of His Word have kept you faithful.

Our God...an Awesome God   4th Bible Reading Marathon

WEEK 15

This Week's Theme:

OUR GOD, A JEALOUS GOD

Dates:

_____ - _____

INSIDE TRACK	MIDDLE LANES	FAST TRACK	
Monday:	**Monday:**	**Monday:**	A Jealous God
☐ Genesis 1:21-27	☐ Exodus 20:1-26	☐ Deuteronomy 6:1-23	
	☐ Exodus 32:1-35	☐ Deuteronomy 13:1-18	
	☐ Isaiah 42:8	☐ Isaiah 1:1-31	
		☐ Revelation 1:8	
		☐ Revelation 4:8	
Tuesday:	**Tuesday:**	**Tuesday:**	Serving God or Man
☐ Matthew 6:11	☐ Luke 6:17-49	☐ John 15:1-17	
	☐ John 3:1-21	☐ Philippians 4:2-20	
	☐	☐ 1 Peter 5:5-11	
		☐ Revelation 12:1-17	
		☐	
Wednesday:	**Wednesday:**	**Wednesday:**	Examples of God's Jealousy
☐ Genesis 12:1-4	☐ Isaiah 54:1-17	☐ Psalm 46:1-11	
	☐ Isaiah 59:1-21	☐ Proverbs 20:1-22	
	☐	☐ Matthew 5:1-48	
		☐ Exodus 34:12-18	
		☐	
Thursday:	**Thursday:**	**Thursday:**	Serving with Heart, Soul and Mind
☐ Genesis 1:28-31	☐ Isaiah 6:1-11	☐ Ecclesiastes 7:1-29	
	☐ Isaiah 25:1-12	☐ Daniel 8:1-27	
	☐	☐ Jeremiah 10:17-25	
		☐ James 2:14-26	
		☐	
Friday:	**Friday:**	**Friday:**	What this Means to us Today
☐ Matthew 7:21-23	☐ Matthew 25:31-46	☐ Romans 12:1-21	
	☐ Matthew 28:16-20	☐ Hebrews 10:19-29	
	☐	☐ 1 John 1:1-29	
		☐	
		☐	

Growing Panes

No. 415

No Other God

The little church in Boswell, Oklahoma, used a songbook that contained a large number of "Stamps/Baxter" type songs. Beautiful songs that were enjoyed by the entire congregation. However, the covers were worn out, and the books were out of print, so the men decided to replace them with *Christian Hymns* compiled by L. O. Sanderson.

After the new hymnals had been in the pews for a couple of weeks, one of the old song leaders came over early on a Sunday morning and replaced all the new hymnals with the old worn out books!

"We've used these books for a hundred years" he argued, "They are a lot better than the new ones!"

The root idea in the Old Testament word *jealous* is to become intensely red. It seems to refer to the changing color of the face or the rising heat of the emotions, which are associated with intense zeal or fervor over something dear to us. We usually think of "jealousy" as a green-eyed monster with overtones of selfishness, suspicion and mistrust.

But, the Bible says our God is a jealous god. His people are "very dear" to him much like a wife is dear to a loving husband (Hosea 2:19). His Name is above every name (Exodus 34:12-14) and is very dear to Him. He will not share his glory with any idol (Isaiah 42:8), including the idols of our hearts.

| Dates: _____-_____ | This Week's Theme: | WEEK 16 |

THE GOD OF OUR SALVATION

INSIDE TRACK	MIDDLE LANES	FAST TRACK	
Monday:	**Monday:**	**Monday:**	God Saves
☐ Acts 4:8-12	☐ 1 Chronicles 16:7-36	☐ 1 Peter 3:15-22	
	☐ John 1:1-34	☐ Psalm 68:19-28	
	☐	☐ Psalm 7:1-17	
		☐ Psalm 55:16-23	
		☐ Zechariah 9:9-17	
Tuesday:	**Tuesday:**	**Tuesday:**	The Power of Salvation
☐ Romans 1:14-16	☐ Psalm 65:1-13	☐ Isaiah 12:1-6	
	☐ Acts 13:26-39	☐ Revelation 12:10-12	
	☐ 1 Peter 1:3-25	☐ Ephesians 1:3-23	
		☐ Revelation 19:1-8	
		☐ Hebrews 1:1-14	
Wednesday:	**Wednesday:**	**Wednesday:**	Saved to Serve
☐ Daniel 3:28	☐ Luke 1:57-80	☐ Acts 2:40-47	
	☐ Daniel 3:1-30	☐ Philippians 2:5-13	
	☐	☐ 2 Peter 3:2-18	
		☐ 1 Peter 3:1-7	
		☐	
Thursday:	**Thursday:**	**Thursday:**	The Saved and the Lost
☐ Mark 16:15-16	☐ 1 Thessalonians 2:1-20	☐ Luke 13:1-30	
	☐ Mark 16:1-20	☐ John 3:26-36	
	☐	☐ 1 Corinthians 1:18-31	
		☐ 1 Corinthians 3:10-17	
		☐ Luke 19:1-10	
Friday:	**Friday:**	**Friday:**	What this Means to us Today
☐ John 3:16-17	☐ Acts 2:14-39	☐ John 3:1-21	
	☐ Acts 13:4-25	☐ Luke 24:44-49	
	☐	☐ 2 Peter 1:2-17	
		☐ 1 Thessalonians 5:4-24	
		☐	

Growing Panes No. 416

The Power of the Word

The old Fifth Avenue church building in Corsicana, Texas, was built in the late 19th century. The 2nd floor auditorium had a balcony that made a complete U-shape above the main floor. A young couple with their two young sons were sitting in the balcony of that building one Sunday morning when the sermon was particularly focused on the urgency of becoming a Christian. The young mother was the only Christian in the family.

When the sermon ended and called for a response, the father very angrily stormed out of his seat, down the stairs, and went outside. Jesse, a deacon and friend, followed and stopped him at the steps and urged him to come back in.

In the meantime, thinking his father was going down to become a Christian, the fourteen-year old son followed his example. When the father came back in, and saw his son on the front pew, he went down also. That day a father and his son experienced salvation, each following the example of the other.

The first converts to Christianity were "pricked in their hearts" (Acts 2). The power and force of the Gospel message moved three thousand to be saved by repenting and being baptized "for the remission" of their sins (Acts 2:38). A new birth is not always without pain.

The rest of the story: Just a few weeks later, the fourteen-year old boy was accidently shot and killed by his nine-year old brother!

Our God...an Awesome God 4th Bible Reading Marathon

WEEK 17

This Week's Theme:

OUR FATHER

Dates: _____ - _____

INSIDE TRACK	Middle Lanes	FAST TRACK	
Monday:	**Monday:**	**Monday:**	Our Father
☐ 1 John 3:1	☐ 1 Chronicles 29:1-20;	☐ Romans 8:12-17	
	☐ Matthew 6:1-34	☐ 2 Samuel 7:12-16	
	☐	☐ John 5:18-30	
		☐	
		☐	
Tuesday:	**Tuesday:**	**Tuesday:**	Who Art in Heaven
☐ Matthew 6:9	☐ Psalm 115:1-18	☐ Matthew 18:10-14	
	☐ Psalm 111:1-7	☐ Matthew 7:7-12	
	☐ Isaiah 63:7-19	☐ Matthew 23:8-12	
		☐ Revelation 4:1-11	
		☐ Revelation 21:1-7	
Wednesday:	**Wednesday:**	**Wednesday:**	Children of God by Faith
☐ Galatians 3:26	☐ Hebrews 11:1-39	☐ 1 Peter 1:3-9	
	☐	☐ 1 Timothy 6:11-16	
	☐	☐ 1 John 5-15	
		☐ Romans 1:8-17	
		☐ Romans 10:5-13	
Thursday:	**Thursday:**	**Thursday:**	Oh, to Be Like Him
☐ Romans 12:1-2	☐ Leviticus 19:1-37	☐ Philippians 3:15	
	☐ Matthew 5:38-48	☐ Philippians 2:1-11	
	☐ 1 Corinthians 15:35-58	☐ Colossians 3:1-25	
		☐ 1 Peter 1:13-23	
		☐	
Friday:	**Friday:**	**Friday:**	What this Means to us Today
☐ 1 Corinthians 8:6	☐ Luke 15:11-31	☐ Luke 6:27-36	
	☐ 1 John 3:2-10	☐ Matthew 5:13-16	
	☐	☐ Ephesians 2:4-10	
		☐ Ephesians 1:3-14	
		☐	

Growing Panes No. 417

Daddy Changed!

Daddy was a common man, much like the rusty metal he worked with as a welder. He grew up on the farm, his father was an itinerant preacher, but he never had much time for religion. He loved to hunt and fish, especially on Sundays. He had the reputation of being an honest man, so his business was successful. He provided well for his family of seven. We had many comforts that others did not have...including the first power lawnmower in our part of town! Daddy took a washing machine motor and welded it to a push mower.

Daddy was a good man, but not a Christian.

That all changed in 1948 after I saw him walk down the aisle at church. Everything changed. When he came home from the welding shop for "dinner" (lunch, today), he always had a prayer

for the food...and also for supper! Instead of taking a noon-day nap in his chair, I remember seeing him sitting there reading his Bible. (When he died we found 54 bibles in his library). He had been a "three-pack-a-day" man, but he quit smoking. And church! It seemed like we started going to church all the time... every Sunday...and Wednesday...and any other time there was a Gospel meeting within a hundred miles!

I think he must have loved us kids more, too, because I remember, after that he hugged us...*actually* hugged us!

All that began to happen after Grandpa's funeral. The Bible says, *And as it is appointed for men to die once, but after this the judgment,"* (Hebrews 9:27). Maybe this is what changed Daddy!

| Dates: _____ - _____ | This Week's Theme:
GOD IS GOOD | | WEEK 18 |

INSIDE TRACK

Monday:
- [ ] Psalm 107:1

Tuesday:
- [ ] Ephesians 2:10

Wednesday:
- [ ] Psalm 141:4

Thursday:
- [ ] 1 Peter 5:7

Friday:
- [ ] Luke 18:19

MIDDLE LANES

Monday:
- [ ] Exodus 33:1-23
- [ ] Mark 10:17-31
- [ ] Psalm 33:5

Tuesday:
- [ ] Romans 2:6-11
- [ ] Galatians 6:1-10
- [ ] Matthew 5:14-16

Wednesday:
- [ ] 1 Corinthians 6:9-11
- [ ] Exodus 20:1-26
- [ ]

Thursday:
- [ ] 1 Peter 5:6-11
- [ ] Luke 4:38-44
- [ ] John 19:17-30

Friday:
- [ ] Romans 11:22
- [ ] Romans 8:28-39
- [ ]

FAST TRACK

Monday:
- [ ] Psalm 107:1-8
- [ ] Genesis 1:31
- [ ] Nahum 1:7
- [ ] Psalm 136:1-26
- [ ] Romans 2:4

Tuesday:
- [ ] James 2:14-26
- [ ] John 6:16-29
- [ ] 2 Timothy 3:14-17
- [ ]
- [ ]

Wednesday:
- [ ] Daniel 9:1-14
- [ ] Romans 1:18-32
- [ ] Ecclesiastes 8:11-13
- [ ]
- [ ]

Thursday:
- [ ] Philippians 2:5-11
- [ ] Matthew 15:29-39
- [ ] Matthew 22:34-40
- [ ]
- [ ]

Friday:
- [ ] Genesis 2:9-25
- [ ] Romans 5:8
- [ ] Psalm 145:9
- [ ] James 1:17
- [ ]

The Goodness of God

Good Works

Evil Works

Does Jesus Care?

What this Means to us Today

God Answers Prayers

Growing Panes No. 418

"There's the handle, the trigger, the barrel, and, finally, the bullet. And when that bullet is fired from the gun, it's going to come out with a speed and power like you've never seen— wham!"

That's how Truman Capote described his unfinished novel, *Answered Prayers,* to *People* magazine. The novel was to be a thinly clad 'expose of New York society. It was not completed before his death, but early installments in *Esquire* had the disturbing impact of a smoking gun. The book was to be based on a quotation from Saint Teresa of Avila: "Answered prayers cause more tears than those that remain unanswered."

Real answered prayers have a similar force. They can move mountains! Win battles! And, bring tears like drops of blood! The adage is so true, "Be careful what you ask for!"

Jesus said that if we continue in a living relationship with Him and *if His Word abides in us,* then our prayers will be answered (1 John 5:14-15). His abiding Word in our hearts actually filters our prayers in accordance with His Word.

But, the Bible says, "One who turns away his ear from hearing the Law, even his prayers shall be an abomination" (Proverbs 28:9). Praying and Bible study go together.

Our God...an Awesome God 4th Bible Reading Marathon

WEEK 19

This Week's Theme:

GOD IS LOVE

Dates:

_____ - _____

INSIDE TRACK	MIDDLE LANES	FAST TRACK	
Monday:	**Monday:**	**Monday:**	God is Love
☐ 1 John 4:8	☐ Psalm 36:6-8	☐ 1 John 4:1-21	
	☐ Psalm 17:6-9	☐	
	☐ Psalm 139:7-12	☐	
		☐	
		☐	
Tuesday:	**Tuesday:**	**Tuesday:**	Examples of the Love of God
☐ Romans 5:8	☐ Psalm 136-2	☐ 1 John 3:16-18	
	☐ Isaiah 41:8-10	☐ Romans 8:35-39	
	☐ Jeremiah 31:3-6	☐ Psalm 103:8-12	
		☐ Psalm 118:5-7	
		☐	
Wednesday:	**Wednesday:**	**Wednesday:**	God so Loved the World
☐ John 3:16	☐ Isaiah 53:4-6	☐ 1 John 3:1-3	
	☐ Isaiah 43:4-5	☐ Ephesians 3:14-19	
	☐	☐ Isaiah 9:6-7	
		☐ John 11:17-37	
		☐	
Thursday:	**Thursday:**	**Thursday:**	Love One Another
☐ Ephesians 4:2	☐ Philippians 2:1-5	☐ Romans 13:8-10	
	☐ 1 John 4:7-12	☐ Galatians 5:13-15	
	☐ John 13:34-35	☐ Mark 12:28-34	
		☐	
		☐	
Friday:	**Friday:**	**Friday:**	What this Means to us Today
☐ Matthew 6:24-25	☐ Matthew 5:43-48	☐ John 15:9-17	
	☐ John 14:21-24	☐ Galatians 2:19-21	
	☐	☐ Ephesians 5:25	
		☐ Psalm 27:1-5	
		☐	

Growing Panes
No. 419

A Son's Love

At his father's funeral, American Carl Lewis placed his 100-meter gold medal from the 1984 Olympics in his father's hands. "Don't worry," he told his surprised mother. "I'll get another one." A year later in the 1988 Olympics, it appeared that Ben Johnson beat him by five feet to win the 100-meter final. Disappointed, Lewis congratulated him with dignity and class. But, following investigations in illegal steroid use, Johnson was stripped of his gold metal. It was given to Carl Lewis.

Partially under the influence of liquor, a man wandered into a religious gathering that had a sign over the door, "God is love." When the meeting was over, everyone left the building except the man who sat there weeping. The preacher walked down to where he was sitting all alone and asked, "What did I say that touched you so tonight?" "Oh..I didn't hear a word you said, it was the sign over the door, '"God is love"'!

The Bible says *"God so loved the world that he gave his one and only son for it"* (John 3:16). That's the extent of our Father's love, shown through His Son.

Love pays off! Of all the Christian virtues we might possess, the greatest is love (1 Corinthians 13). Real love is unconditional. God loved us even while we were (are) sinners (Romans 5:8). Love functions even when the "odds" of race, color, or creed magnify our differences.

Dates:	This Week's Theme:		
_____ - _____	**GOD IS MERCIFUL**		**WEEK 20**

INSIDE TRACK	**MIDDLE LANES**	**FAST TRACK**	
Monday:	**Monday:**	**Monday:**	**The Mercy of God**
☐ Psalm 37:25-26	☐ Psalm 4:1-3	☐ Luke 1:46-55	
	☐ Numbers 14:17-19	☐ Galatians 6:16	
	☐ Deuteronomy 21:8-9	☐	
		☐	
		☐	
Tuesday:	**Tuesday:**	**Tuesday:**	**Mercy and Justice**
☐ Proverbs 3:3	☐ Proverbs 14:22	☐ Nehemiah 8:13-18	
	☐ Proverbs 21:21	☐ Psalm 18:25-29	
	☐ Hosea 14:4-7	☐	
		☐	
		☐	
Wednesday:	**Wednesday:**	**Wednesday:**	**His Mercy Illustrated**
☐ Luke 17:13	☐ 1 Corinthians 7:25	☐ 2 Samuel 7:1-16	
	☐ 2 Corinthians 4:1	☐ Psalm 41:4-12	
	☐ James 2:13	☐	
		☐	
		☐	
Thursday:	**Thursday:**	**Thursday:**	**Mercy and Forgiveness**
☐ Deuteronomy 13:17 -18	☐ Psalm 99:8-9	☐ John 21:15-23	
	☐ Psalm 130:3-5	☐ Psalm 123:3-4	
	☐ Colossians 1:13-23	☐ Luke 6:36	
		☐ Matthew 5:7	
		☐	
Friday:	**Friday:**	**Friday:**	**What this Means to us Today**
☐ Matthew 6:14	☐ Mark 2:1-5	☐ Psalm 103:3-6	
	☐ 1 Peter 5:6-9	☐ Ephesians 2:3-10	
	☐ Psalm 57:9-11	☐ Colossians 3:12	
		☐ 2 Peter 3:9	
		☐ Micah 6:8	

Growing Panes

No. 420

We *Deserve* Justice, We *Need* Mercy

The little three year old found a bottle of Old English furniture polish under the kitchen sink and drank some of it. Her young mother found her unconscious on the kitchen floor. She was rushed to the hospital, but she died two days later.

A small Oklahoma church was literally torn apart by this incident. Two prominent families, members of that church, were angered and saddened by what had happened. The young father and his family blamed the mother for the tragic accident for "not properly supervising" the little girl. The father was accused of "never being home, always out hunting." Cruel, hard words passed between their families.

Later, the mother attempted suicide. The young couple eventually divorced. Both of them dropped out of church.

Guilt can be terrifying! We know God holds us accountable for our sins, so we desperately try to place blame. The word "justice" demands what all of us deserve, blame! We are guilty.

John saw God on His thundering throne of justice high and lifted up (Revelation 4). However, the Bible also tells us that "a rainbow was round about the throne." This could be a symbol of God's loving mercy.

Our actions, careless or intentional, *will* bring consequences. But our God always provides a brighter day after the storm and certifies it with "the rainbow" of His mercy.

WEEK 21

This Week's Theme:

GOD IS JUST

Dates:

_____ - _____

INSIDE TRACK	MIDDLE LANES	FAST TRACK	
Monday:	**Monday:**	**Monday:**	A Just God
☐ 2 Thessalonians 1:6	☐ Deuteronomy 32:41-43	☐ Revelation 19:1-8	
	☐ Psalm 74:22-23	☐ Deuteronomy 27:1-8	
	☐ Isaiah 49:22-26	☐ Malachi 2:10-17	
		☐ Amos 5:14	
		☐ Micah 6:1-8	
Tuesday:	**Tuesday:**	**Tuesday:**	God's Law and Grace
☐ Exodus 23:22	☐ Psalm 79:10-12	☐ Daniel 9:4-19	
	☐ Zechariah 2:7-9	☐ 2 Chronicles 9:1-12	
	☐ Revelation 11:15-19	☐ 1 Kings 10:9	
		☐ Job 30:1-31	
		☐ Isaiah 66:24	
Wednesday:	**Wednesday:**	**Wednesday:**	His Justice Illustrated
☐ Ecclesiastes 3:17	☐ Psalm 94:20-23	☐ Isaiah 30:15-18	
	☐ Revelation 6:1-11	☐ Psalm 99:4-5	
	☐ Genesis 41:25-40	☐ 2 Thessalonians 1:8-9	
		☐ Deuteronomy 10:12-22	
		☐	
Thursday:	**Thursday:**	**Thursday:**	The Judgment of God
☐ Jeremiah 50:29	☐ Revelation 15:1-4	☐ Isaiah 61:7-9	
	☐ Exodus 8:16-19	☐ Psalm 9:7-8	
	☐ Revelation 18:17-24	☐ Psalm 140:12-13	
		☐ 1 Samuel 24:1-22	
		☐ Romans 12:17-21	
Friday:	**Friday:**	**Friday:**	What this Means to us Today
☐ Colossians 3:25	☐ Deuteronomy 16:18-21	☐ Deuteronomy 32:1-4	
	☐ Luke 16:1-15	☐ Revelation 20:11-15	
	☐ 2 Chronicles 19:4-11	☐ Job 34:10-20	
		☐ Revelation 16:5-6	
		☐	

Growing Panes No. 421

Let God be the Judge

He was a serial killer and sex offender, who raped and murdered seventeen men and boys between 1978 and 1991. Yet, Jeffrey Dahmer requested to be baptized while in prison. He was baptized by Roy Ratcliff on May 10, 1994. Ratcliff tells the story of how that came about in *Dark Journey, Deep Grace*.

His conversion sparked hot debates among both religious zealots and secular pundits. Dahmer was bludgeoned to death by fellow inmate Christopher Scarver on November 28, 1994. One theologian said, "If Jeffrey Dahmer is in heaven, I don't want to go there!"

While vacationing in Wisconsin, we visited the services of the Madison church of Christ. Roy Ratcliff was speaking that day. Following his lesson, we talked at some length about "Jeffrey Dah-

mer." He told how Curt Booth, a prison minister in Oklahoma, made contact with Dahmer and sent him a Bible correspondence course. After studying, he requested to be baptized. Booth called several preachers in the area before he found one who was willing to go into the prison and talk with Dahmer. After several in-prison Bible studies, arrangements were made for the baptism.

Most of us abhor such evil actions! I told Ratcliff that he deserved more than just death.

"Yes," he responded, "that would be justice." But he continued, "As a Christian you have to ask yourself just how effective is the Grace of God? Is the blood of Christ strong enough to save someone who has done such gruesome things?" Good question. Justice without mercy *is* terrible!

Dates:	This Week's Theme:	
_____-_____	**GOD IS FORGIVING**	**WEEK 22**

INSIDE TRACK

Monday:
- [ ] John 1:9

Tuesday:
- [ ] Hebrews 8:12

Wednesday:
- [ ] Matthew 6:14-15

Thursday:
- [ ] Psalm 99:8

Friday:
- [ ] Romans 8:28

MIDDLE LANES

Monday:
- [ ] Psalm 32:1-11
- [ ] John 3:16-21
- [ ] Matthew 9:1-8

Tuesday:
- [ ] Ephesians 4:1-32
- [ ] 2 Chronicles 7:11-18
- [ ]

Wednesday:
- [ ] Romans 4:1-25
- [ ] Psalm 99:1-9
- [ ] Galatians 5:19-26

Thursday:
- [ ] Luke 15:11-32
- [ ] Matthew 5:21-26
- [ ]

Friday:
- [ ] Mark 7:14-29
- [ ] Mark 9:42-50
- [ ] Luke 15:1-7

FAST TRACK

Monday:
- [ ] Acts 2:1-41
- [ ]
- [ ]
- [ ]
- [ ]

Tuesday:
- [ ] Luke 23:1-43
- [ ]
- [ ]
- [ ]
- [ ]

Wednesday:
- [ ] Ephesians 2:1-10
- [ ] Acts 17:3-31
- [ ]
- [ ]
- [ ]

Thursday:
- [ ] Matthew 18:1-35
- [ ] 2 Corinthians 2:1-11
- [ ]
- [ ]
- [ ]

Friday:
- [ ] Matthew 6:1-14
- [ ] Colossians 3:1-17
- [ ] Romans 13:1-14
- [ ]

God Forgives Sins

Examples of God's Forgiveness

God's Conditions for Forgiveness

Our Forgiveness of Others

What this Means to us Today

Growing Panes No. 422

Our God Forgives

The first call came from a leader in the church asking if I remembered a certain man. I said that I did. He had admitted to sinful sexual conduct with at least two members of a church where I was the young preacher. I gave the church leader the details as I remembered them after more than fifty years! So far as I could tell, the man had repented and confessed the sins.

The second call came from one of his victims. Now a woman in her sixties, she was sexually assaulted by him when she was a teenager. The damage done by the assault was more than she was able to bear. Even after more than five decades the pain of that experience seemed to be dictating her life. The man claimed to be a Christian and was a leader in the local church. Although he was now a "working, faithful member" (to quote that leader), she did not believe the church should extend fellowship to such a person.

Someone has accurately described the damaging effects of such a situation: *"Refusing to forgive is the poison we drink hoping someone else will die."* We should base our forgiveness on what God has done for us rather than on what others have *done to* us. (Matthew 6:14-15; Luke 17:3-4).

This trait of our God is clear: *Be kind to one another, tenderhearted, forgiving one another, as God in Christ forgave you.* (Ephesians 4:32 ESV).

WEEK 23

This Week's Theme:

GOD IS FAITHFUL

Dates:

_____ - _____

INSIDE TRACK	MIDDLE LANES	FAST TRACK	
Monday:	**Monday:**	**Monday:**	God is Predictable
☐ 2 Peter 3:8-9	☐ Luke 15:11-24;32	☐ Proverbs 28:13	
	☐ Leviticus 26:40-45	☐ Isaiah 51:1-4	
	☐ Acts 2:36-39	☐ John 3:16-18	
		☐ John 6:37-40	
		☐ Titus 3:3-8	
Tuesday:	**Tuesday:**	**Tuesday:**	Faithfulness Defined
☐ Deuteronomy 7:7-9	☐ Genesis 17:1-9	☐ Deuteronomy 10:12-15	
	☐ Hebrews 11:8-12	☐ Deuteronomy 30:11-20	
	☐ Hebrews 11:17-30	☐ Numbers 23:19	
		☐ Psalm 36:5-9	
		☐ Psalm 33:4-5	
Wednesday:	**Wednesday:**	**Wednesday:**	Same Yesterday, Today and Tomorrow
☐ Psalm 30:5	☐ Exodus 32:1-18	☐ Psalm 103:8-18	
	☐ Exodus 34:5-7	☐ Psalm 25:8-15	
	☐	☐ 1 Peter 1:13-16	
		☐ Jude 1:5-7	
		☐	
Thursday:	**Thursday:**	**Thursday:**	Temptations and God's Faithfulness
☐ 1 Corinthians 10:13	☐ 2 Chronicles 32:2-19	☐ Psalm 46:1-5	
	☐ Isaiah 37:1-20	☐ Mark 14:37-38	
	☐ Isaiah 37:33-38	☐ 2 Peter 2:7-10	
		☐ Hebrews 2:17-18	
		☐ James 1:12-18	
Friday:	**Friday:**	**Friday:**	What this Means to us Today
☐ John 14:23-27	☐ Matthew 25:14-30	☐ Ezekiel 34:17-31	
	☐ Matthew 25:31-46	☐ Hebrews 10:23-25	
	☐ John 17:20-23	☐ Romans 11:33-36	
		☐ Ephesians 3:16-21	
		☐ Galatians 6:7-10	

Growing Pains No. 423

Loving God - *Unconditionally*

Dave appeared to be a faithful husband for many years, but looks can be deceiving. True faithfulness is a matter of both the actions in our lives and the motivations of our hearts. Neither of these defined the events that followed.

Dave had called to ask if I would perform the "renewal wedding-vows ceremony" for he and his wife on their 50th wedding anniversary. A Saturday later a few neighbors, several friends from church and relatives gathered in their backyard to celebrate their fifty years of marriage. It was a beautiful statement about the love of marital bliss. But it was all a lie!

The next morning Dave's wife called and asked if I had seen him. No, I had not. He left immediately after the renewal cele-

bration and did not come back.

Long story – *short!* Dave, a traveling salesman, had a longtime girlfriend in another city. Two weeks later it was discovered that he had moved in with the girlfriend and left his wife of 50 years!

The Bible says, "*Now, Israel, what does the LORD your God require from you, but to fear the LORD your God, to walk in all His ways and love Him, and to serve the LORD your God with all your heart and with all your soul, and to keep the LORD'S commandments and His statutes which I am commanding you today for your good?* (Deuteronomy 10:12-13)

The Bible teaches, "Be faithful," for our God is faithful.

Dates: _____ - _____	This Week's Theme:

A GOD OF GRACE

WEEK 24

INSIDE TRACK

Monday:
- [ ] Romans 11:6

Tuesday:
- [ ] Luke 2:40

Wednesday:
- [ ] 1 Thessalonians 5:28

Thursday:
- [ ] Colossians 4:18

Friday:
- [ ] 1 Peter 5:12

MIDDLE LANES

Monday:
- [ ] Romans 11:1-6
- [ ] Romans 1:7
- [ ] 1 Corinthians 1:3-4

Tuesday:
- [ ] Romans 5:15-17
- [ ] 1 Corinthians 1:4-9
- [ ] 1 Corinthians 15:8-11

Wednesday:
- [ ] 2 Thessalonians 3:13-18
- [ ] 2 Corinthians 8:10-15
- [ ] 2 Corinthians 12:1-10

Thursday:
- [ ] 2 Timothy 4:6-22
- [ ] Titus 3:12-15
- [ ] Hebrews 13:17-25

Friday:
- [ ] 2 Peter 3:17-18
- [ ] Revelation 1:4-7
- [ ] Proverbs 3:1-12

FAST TRACK

Monday:
- [ ] 2 Corinthians 1:2-7
- [ ] Galatians 1:3-9
- [ ] Ephesians 1:2-10
- [ ] Philippians 1:2-11
- [ ] Colossians 1:2-8

Tuesday:
- [ ] 2 Corinthians 8:1-9
- [ ] Romans 5:18-6:4
- [ ] Romans 16:17-20
- [ ] 1 Corinthians 16:13-23
- [ ] Philippians 4:21-23

Wednesday:
- [ ] 2 Corinthians 13:5-14
- [ ] Galatians 5:2-6
- [ ] Ephesians 2:1-10
- [ ] Ephesians 4:7-16
- [ ] Ephesians 6:21-24

Thursday:
- [ ] Titus 1:4-9
- [ ] 2 John 3
- [ ] Hebrews 12:18-29
- [ ] 1 Timothy 1:1-4
- [ ] 2 Timothy 1:1-2

Friday:
- [ ] James 4:1-12
- [ ] Zechariah 4:6-10
- [ ] Zechariah 12:10-14
- [ ] John 1:16-18
- [ ] Acts 4:32-35

Selected by the Grace of God

The Grace of God Upon Us

The Grace of our Lord Jesus Christ

God's Grace Be with You

What this Means to us Today

Growing Panes

No. 424

"Running from the Crabgrass"

I had gone to the farm store in Omaha to purchase something to kill out the crabgrass in my lawn. I wanted my lawn to be beautiful, but the crabgrass was overtaking it. I explained my mission to the ambitious clerk.

"Well," the good-intentioned clerk said, "Crabgrass grows everywhere. It can kill any other grass. Even if you kill the top blades, the roots are still there."

"Besides that," he continued, "the grass produces millions of very small seeds that remain dormant in the ground for years, ready to sprout when the early rains come."

I listened, and thought, "Maybe I should just sell the property and move!" I needed help, but you can't run from crabgrass.

That's the way sin is in my life. It seems to take over. But, there is victory over this aggressive weed found in a knowledge of the Bible. His Word hidden deep in our hearts (Psalms 119:11) makes us aware of sin, spiritually strong and keeps us from sliding down the slippery slope of sin.

In the front of our children's first Bibles, we wrote: "*This Book will keep you from sin, and only sin will keep you from this Book.*"

WEEK 25

This Week's Theme:

GOD IS A SPIRIT

Dates:
_____ - _____

INSIDE TRACK	MIDDLE LANES	FAST TRACK	
Monday:	**Monday:**	**Monday:**	God is a Spirit, not Flesh
☐ Genesis 1:1-2	☐ Numbers 11:24-30	☐ Psalm 139:1-12	
	☐ 1 Samuel 10:1-11	☐ John 4:21-24	
	☐ Matthew 3:13-17	☐ 1 Corinthians 2:6-16	
		☐ 2 Corinthians 3:12-18	
		☐ 1 John 4:7-16	
Tuesday:	**Tuesday:**	**Tuesday:**	Jesus was Flesh and Spirit
☐ John 1:14	☐ Luke 1:26-38	☐ John 1:1-18	
	☐ Luke 4:16-21	☐ John 6:53-65	
	☐ Colossians 2:9-10	☐ John 14:9-14	
		☐ Philippians 2:5-11	
		☐ 1 John 4:1-3	
Wednesday:	**Wednesday:**	**Wednesday:**	Spiritual Blessings
☐ Ephesians 1:3	☐ John 14:15-21	☐ Romans 8:28-39	
	☐ Romans 6:1-11	☐ 2 Corinthians 1:3-7	
	☐ Ephesians 1:3-14	☐ 2 Thessalonians 2:13-17	
		☐ Hebrews 8:10-13	
		☐ 1 Peter 1:3-9	
Thursday:	**Thursday:**	**Thursday:**	Sins of the Flesh
☐ Galatians 5:19-21, 24	☐ Proverbs 6:16-19	☐ Galatians 6:7-10	
	☐ Romans 6:11-14	☐ Ephesians 2:1-10	
	☐ Romans 8:5-17	☐ Ephesians 4:25-32	
		☐ Ephesians 5:3-5	
		☐ Colossians 3:1-17	
Friday:	**Friday:**	**Friday:**	What this Means to us Today
☐ Luke 11:40	☐ Genesis 2:7	☐ 1 Corinthians 15:35-57	
	☐ Matthew 10:26-30	☐ Philippians 3:20, 21	
	☐ 2 Corinthians 5:1-5	☐ 1 Thessalonians 5:23, 24	
		☐ Hebrews 2:14-18	
		☐	

Growing Panes

No. 425

Spirit-filled Living with the Word of God

I stepped into the elevator at Rock Island General Hospital on my way to visit a sick friend. At the same time another man dressed similar to me (suit and tie) hopped in. He looked at me and said, "You must be a minister."

"Yes," I replied wondering how he could tell. "I am going to visit a friend who recently had surgery, and what about you?" I asked assuming he also was a visiting minister.

"I am here to visit, but I don't know who I will visit yet," he said, "I just stand in front of the elevator door for each floor and let the Spirit tell me when to get off."

The Bible says we are to be "filled with the Spirit" (Ephesians 5:18-19), but it also says that we should "let the word of Christ dwell in us with wisdom and teaching" (Colossians 3:16). There are those who think like the minister in the elevator story, to just wait for the Spirit to speak to them in some still small voice.

But, read and compare the two passages noted above. They are very similar. The obvious truth is that a major key to living a "spirit-filled" life and being full of the Holy Spirit is to saturate yourself with the Word of God.

Our God...an Awesome God **4th Bible Reading Marathon**

Racing for the Finish Line...

Peter and Paul were very different.

We remember Peter for his blatant denial of Christ. Paul was the determined rabbi who stood up against both his former brethren and the heathen Roman court. Peter is known by the foot-in-the-mouth occasions when he impetuously spoke when he should have remained silent. Paul was actually "Dr." Paul! In today's world he would be the well-educated professor who says exactly what he means with a clear command of his grammar. Peter stood in Jerusalem and delivered the first gospel sermon; Paul (rather, *Saul!*) stood over the body of the first Christian to die for the faith. Peter's background was that of a fisherman. Paul had credentials that would have been accepted in the finest circles of his day.

But, in addition to that, Paul did not have the blessing of three years of personal contact with our Lord. He "met" him on the road to Damascus, was soon taught and baptized by Ananias in Damascus. Peter was called directly by Jesus with the simple words, "Follow me." Paul's calling was with bright lights, erotic sounds and mysterious visions.

Different as they were at first, they look almost alike near the ends of their journeys!

Peter's last days are most vividly given in prophecy by Jesus himself (John 21:15-19). Jesus compelled Peter to think about the end with the piercing question: "*Simon, son of Jonah, do you love me more than these?*" This was the third time Jesus had been seen by Peter since his resurrection, and he asked the question three times: "*Do you love me?*" Each time Peter answered, "*Lord, you know I love you.*" Three times Jesus responded, "*Feed my sheep!*" Paul's last days are chronicled in the trials he experienced as a prisoner and opportunities to preach even in Rome. Most of the book of Acts gives a detailed history of his end.

But the pages of inspiration fall silent on the very last days for both men. Tradition says Paul was executed in the city of Rome and that Peter, upon his request, was crucified upside down!

Paul perhaps spoke for both of these loyal disciples of Christ when he told Timothy,

> "*I have fought the good fight, I have finished the race, I have kept the faith. Finally, there is laid up for me the crown of righteousness, which the Lord, the righteous judge, will give to me on that Day, and not to me only but also to all who have loved His appearing. (2 Timothy 4:7-8)*

You are reaching the end of this Bible Reading Marathon. We have come a long way together in searching out the nature and character of our God. Many direct commands have been studied. Even more lessons have been learned from the biblical examples we have read. Our God is truly an awesome God who loves us! The Bible says, "*If you love me, keep my commandments*" (John 14:15)

Now, the same question our Lord asked Peter could be asked of us: "*Do you love me more than these?*" Each of us want to respond as Paul did in his final letter to Timothy, "*I have fought a good fight, I have finished the race, I have kept the faith..*" Like Paul and Peter, we anticipate and look forward to a crown of righteousness! That's why knowing about our awesome God is so important!

WEEK 26

This Week's Theme:

BEWARE OF FALSE GODS

Dates: _____ - _____

INSIDE TRACK	MIDDLE LANES	FAST TRACK	
Monday:	**Monday:**	**Monday:**	One True God
☐ Exodus 20:2-3	☐ 1 Kings 18:15-39	☐ Exodus 20:4-26	
	☐ Daniel 6:1-28	☐ Matthew 4:1-11	
	☐ Judges 6:1-40	☐ Isaiah 43:1-11	
		☐ Isaiah 44:1-8	
		☐ Romans 1:18-20	
Tuesday:	**Tuesday:**	**Tuesday:**	Idol Worship Illustrated
☐ Leviticus 26:1	☐ 1 Samuel 5:1-12	☐ Psalm 115:2-8	
	☐ Ezekiel 14:1-11	☐ Jeremiah 10:1-16	
	☐ 2 Chronicles 24:1-27	☐ Acts 17:22-31	
		☐ Colossians 3:1-14	
		☐ Ephesians 5:1-7	
Wednesday:	**Wednesday:**	**Wednesday:**	Gods of This World
☐ James 4:2-4	☐ 2 Kings 17:1-20	☐ Matthew 15:8-9	
	☐ 2 Peter 2:1-22	☐ Colossians 2:16-19	
	☐	☐ Romans 1:21-32	
		☐ 1 John 4:1-19	
		☐ 2 Corinthians 4:1-6	
Thursday:	**Thursday:**	**Thursday:**	Fellowship with God
☐ 1 John 1:5-7	☐ Joshua 24:1-27	☐ Jeremiah 9:23-24	
	☐ 1 Corinthians 10:1-13	☐ 1 John 1:8-10	
	☐ 1 Corinthians 13:1-8	☐ 1 John 2:1-17	
		☐ 1 John 3:7-10	
		☐ 2 Corinthians 6:16-18	
Friday:	**Friday:**	**Friday:**	What this Means to us Today
☐ John 14:6	☐ 1 Kings 11:1-6	☐ Colossians 2:20-23	
	☐ 2 Timothy 3:1-9	☐ 1 Corinthians 10:14-33	
	☐ Romans 12:1-21	☐ 1 Timothy 6:6-10	
		☐ Revelation 21:22-27	
		☐ Matthew 22:34-40	

Growing Panes No. 426

"This *is* My Father's World!"

I've heard that our sense of smell is most closely associated with memory. The smell of rain does take me back to my childhood days in Oklahoma. All of my senses were alert, I remember, when we would sit on the back porch and watch it rain. We could smell the fresh rainwater while we listened to the rain pelting the tin roof.

The sweet smell and sights of flowers, especially roses, remind me of the times I watched my daddy hoe his rose garden. So many of my good childhood memories are prompted by the sights, sounds, and smells of God's wonderful world.

But a dark cloud that boils with thunder and lightning triggers a different memory. My mind goes back to April 12, 1945. At 5:45, one of the most devastating tornadoes in the history of the state of Oklahoma struck the little town of Antlers. That ugly mass of swirling air used the same elements of God's world to bring death and destruction. God's beautiful largest trees were reduced to splinters. The landscape of His world took on the sight, sound and smell of death. Seventy-four people died that day. More than 1,500 people were left homeless!

The very nature of God's world invites imitation gods drawn from that world. The Bible lists nearly three dozen false gods by name, not to mention the un-named gods of money and fame. There were so many false gods in Athens that one was called the "unknown god" just in case they missed one (Acts 17:23).

Remember: False "gods" look like the real "God"...made from His creation!

Test Yourself...(*Questions compiled from 26-week Reading Schedule*)

1) At the burning bush Moses was told to:
   a) Standup and be a man
   b) Bow his head in humility
   c) Take off his shoes

2) His name was changed to "Israel" to signify that God is almighty:
   a) Abraham
   b) Jacob
   c) Joseph

3) Heaven and earth may pass away, but these will never pass away:
   a) Moon and stars
   b) God's words
   c) Ten Commandments

4) Circumcision was first instituted through the male descendants of this man as a sign of the covenant between God and his people:
   a) Noah
   b) Moses
   c) Abraham

5) A city where man's tendency to create his own god resulted in the creation of many gods, even an "unknown god".
   a) Athens
   b) Rome
   c) Babylon

6) A young man who was found guilty of breaking the law by praying to god, his Lord and Master:
   a) David
   b) Daniel
   c) Darius

7) He told Samuel, "I have sinned because I feared the people and obeyed their voice" and was removed as King.
   a) Saul
   b) Jehosophat
   c) Ahab

8) The Lord , my Shepherd leads me in the paths of righteousness:
   a) To find water
   b) Because he loves me
   c) For His name's sake

9) A woman was healed by the great physician when she:
   a) Was called a dog
   b) Touched his clothes
   c) Yelled out above the crowd

10) Jonah tried to get out of the presence of God by running to:
    a) Nineveh
    b) Tarshish
    c) Damascus

11) Paul said he was not ashamed of the gospel because:
    a) It is the good news
    b) Shows the love of God
    c) It is the power of God

12) Jesus told of a Pharisee and a tax collector to teach a lesson about:
    a) Duties as citizens
    b) Prayer and humility
    c) Going to church regularly

13) Jesus taught "I am the way, the truth and the life:
    a) And the Way is hard
    b) I am the only way to God
    c) And I won't die

14) Hannah, the mother of Samuel, prayed for a son. If her prayer was answered, she promised to:
    a) Be faithful all her life
    b) Give him to the Lord
    c) Raise him to be faithful

15) The prophet Hosea was taught about this trait of God when he was told to take a wife:
    a) A just God
    b) A jealous God
    c) A joyous God

16) Disciples of Jesus are told to go into all the world and
    a) Preach the gospel
    b) Do good to all men
    c) Feed and clothe the needy

17) We are God's children, therefore we are:
    a) Safe from all harm
    b) Heirs of God
    c) Abbas

18) Jesus fed more than 4000 with a few fish and how many loaves of bread?
    a) 5
    b) 6
    c) 7

19) God loved us when we were:
    a) Trying to be good
    b) Sinners
    c) Being persecuted

20) David said he had been young and now was old but he had never seen the righteous forsaken, or their:
    a) children disobedient
    b) children hungry
    c) children begging bread

21) The Bible teaches that vengeance belongs to:
    a) The elder son
    b) Anyone
    c) God

22) How many times should we forgive our brother who sins against us?
    a) One time only
    b) Three times
    c) Seven times or more

23) How far will God allow a person to be tempted?
    a) Not beyond what you can bear
    b) Until you break
    c) Until it is painful

24) Saved by the grace of God
    a) Unconditionally
    b) Conditioned on faith alone
    c) Conditioned on faith and obedience

25) The Word became
    a) God
    b) Flesh
    c) The Bible

26) False teachers come in sheep's clothing, but inwardly are
    a) Wolves
    b) Angels
    c) Disciples

Answers to "Test Yourself": 1. c; 2. b; 3. b; 4. c; 5. a; 6. b; 7. a; 8.c; 9.b; 10. b; 11. c; 12. b;13. b;14. b; 15. b; 16. a;17. b; 18. a;
19. b; 20. c; 21. c; 22. c; 23. a; 24. c, 25. b; 26. a;

Notes on your Readings

Notes on your Readings

www.ingramcontent.com/pod-product-compliance
Lightning Source LLC
Chambersburg PA
CBHW041221040426

42443CB00002B/37